FORBES FIELD, PITTSBURGH | *October 13, 1960*

Sports Illustrated

THE STORY OF

Baseball

IN 100 PHOTOGRAPHS

CONTENTS

KOSTYA KENNEDY *Editor* | BILL SYKEN *Writer*
MIRIAM MARSEU *Photo Editor* | ERIC MARQUARD *Designer* | KEVIN KERR *Copy Editor*
STEFANIE KAUFMAN *Project Manager* | DAN LARKIN *Premedia Senior Manager*

PLAY AT THE PLATE | *Fenway Park, Boston, 1937*

BEING THERE

by KOSTYA KENNEDY

THE FIRST CELEBRATED PHOTOGRAPHS taken in the United States—among them portraits of former President John Quincy Adams and President James Polk—were shot in the 1840s, which was right about the time that the first organized baseball games, staged in front of audiences and guided by essentially the same rules that guide the game today, were being played. In the years and decades that followed, photography blossomed in popularity. Technique improved. Photo studios proliferated. Prominent folks sat to have their portraits taken. Baseball was blossoming in popularity as well, in various regions of the country and across social strata, at once a genteel sport for gentlemen seeking wholesome exercise, and a more rough-edged enterprise attracting young, hard-nosed athletes to the field as well as gamblers, among many others, to the sidelines. ❧ By the time the Cincinnati Red Stockings debuted as the first openly professional baseball team, in 1869, America's growing young sport was already known as the national pastime. The Red Stockings traveled from coast to coast and were enormously successful, winning convincingly and with aplomb. Thousands of fans turned out to watch and to cheer. The team was clearly onto something, so it stood to reason that that summer—with portraiture still the most dominant of photographic endeavors, and one that conveyed a sense of importance to its subjects—the Red Stockings would go to a studio and hold their collective pose. For the famous Civil War photographer Mathew Brady no less. The players didn't smile much. Nobody smiled for photographs in those days. But as the Red Stockings stood and stared into the lens, the era of baseball photography surely, if stoically, got under way.

There had certainly been *images* of baseball before Cincinnati's team portrait, notably the Brueghel-esque color lithograph at right, of Union prisoners playing the game in 1862 under Confederate guard at a camp in North Carolina. Soldiers often played ball during the Civil War (that's part of what led the sport to expand when the armies dispersed at war's end) and team rivalries were fierce. The artist, a Prussian-born captain and sometime painter named Otto Boetticher, captured the game in mid-dalliance: the pitcher about to unleash the ball, a runner taking off to steal second base. It was a scene rich in nuance and detail, a ball-field moment

On-field photographers sometimes got tangled up with fielders, or overheard conversations the league would have rathered they had not.

the likes of which photographers would not capture until many decades later.

Photo-wise, the first half century of professional baseball's century-and-a-half life consists primarily of players posed (for tobacco cards sometimes) or going through rudimentary paces on the grass, not much in the way of real action. From 1903 emerges a memorable (if grainy) photograph showing the scene and the crowd at the inaugural World Series in Boston but little from those Series games themselves. Evocative action photos weren't really taken at a World Series until 1919, as the scene of the Reds' Greasy Neale sliding into second base on the following page shows. (Of course we remember that Series for something else entirely, and for Shoeless

Joe Jackson, who appears on page 38 among the 100 photos included here to tell the story of the sport.) More frequent in those years were renderings of a star standing on the sideline, perhaps tossing a ball or idly swinging a bat. From this fare, some telling pictures do survive: The broad and powerful Cy Young in late career, say, or Big Train Walter Johnson, his jaw prominent, his long right arm swept across his body, his eyes lidded from the sun, looking every bit the seminal fastballer. The action photographs of that era, such as Wee Willie Keeler at the bat, hitting 'em where they warn't in 1908, or, more magnificently, Ty Cobb coming hard and hell-bent into third base, in 1910, his slide spraying dirt and fairly splitting the third baseman in two, well, such

photographs remain rare jewels to be treasured, much like those players themselves.

THE PUBLIC'S APPETITE for photography (both as documentation and as art) only deepened and so too did the public's appetite for baseball. Ballpark attendance jumped by more than 50% from the 1910s to the 1920s. (Thanks, Babe.) Radio broadcasts began and eventually became more common. Television arrived. People not only wanted to see the games and their diamond heroes, but they also wanted to savor them. There was a time, during the '30s and '40s and on into the '50s too, when Major League Baseball allowed photographers onto the field of play, in foul grounds just 10 or 15 feet up the

baseline from home plate. They would stand, undaunted and unafraid, like members of a gallery at the tee, and fix their cameras upon the batter in the box. They were in good position too, for when a player came 'round and crossed home plate.

The practice of allowing on-field photography went away, in part because photographers sometimes got tangled up with fielders on foul balls, and in part because these picture-snapping newsmen would sometimes overhear conversations that the league brass would just as soon they hadn't. (Reds manager Birdie Tebbetts to umpire Bill Stewart, via AP photographer Gene Smith: "You're a lousy umpire. . . . Why don't you quit?") Besides, the need for such proximity lessened

WORLD SERIES, GAME 2 | *Redland Field, Cincinnati, 1919*

with the development of more powerful and subtle camera equipment. Yet for all the gorgeous pictures photographers were delivering, in black-and-white, in color, there were so many ordinary ones too. Even in the modern game, and even with those more modern (even ultramodern) resources, capturing the truly superior action photo remained, and remains, elusive. It's the nature of the sport and of the discipline.

"When you're shooting baseball, you're waiting. You're waiting and you're attentive," says Ronald C. Modra, who covered the game for SPORTS ILLUSTRATED for 25 years. "Something extraordinary is going to happen, but you don't know when or where. You make your best calculations. When I was shooting the Yankees in the early '80s I used to stay focused on [third baseman] Graig Nettles when a righthanded hitter came up for the other team. Nettles was so athletic and dynamic as a fielder, you figured there was a chance something beautiful would happen. But of course you never knew. The truth was if you got one or two really good or possibly great photos you felt like it was a good day."

Images, even attractive and revealing ones, can feel common these days, an era in which a cellphone trained from the stadium seats can bring a pitcher's mid-windup expression into focus. And yet the transcendent image—that which begins to tell a story of the thing itself, and of the environment around the thing, and of other, related things too—those images are rare. Willie Mays making his over-the-shoulder catch in 1954. Bill Mazeroski arriving home—floating, really—on the winds of his home run that won the '60 World Series. Carlton Fisk waving his long ball fair in '75. Rickey Henderson churning to second base in '92. Moises Alou, interrupted, in 2003. Bryce Harper bristling in dirt-stained, unshaven intensity during his 2015 season for the ages.

The action is not always where it's at. Some of the most moving baseball photos take in moments of other enterprise. Lou Gehrig, his head bowed in stoic speech, 1939. Roger Maris, smoking alone in the clubhouse in the late summer of '61. Roberto Clemente in portrait, 1970. Ozzie Smith in mid-air, 1985. Theo Epstein in dialogue with Billy Beane, 2010. Each of the 100 photos that drive this book's narrative tells a discrete story, even as it fits into a larger story as well, reaching forward, reaching back.

During spring training of 1986, Modra took a photograph of Ted Williams sitting at a restaurant table

PETE ROSE | *Wrigley Field, Chicago, 1975*

with Wade Boggs and Don Mattingly. It appears on page 156. Boggs had just won the second of what would be five batting titles. Mattingly was the reigning American League MVP. Williams is the best hitter since Babe Ruth.

The players are talking technique, naturally, as Williams's half-swing gesture implies. Boggs and Mattingly are both turned to look at him, locked in. There's more. Williams, at 67, has forearms as thick as thighs. The table is lousy with glasses. Shrimp has been eaten. Williams has a white cloth napkin tucked like a bib into the collar of his shirt. The younger men do not. "That was the detail that made it for me," says Modra. "The napkin. The different generations. It somehow brought it all together."

EVEN THE MOST memorable photographs have their borders, limits upon what they might communicate and how they might communicate it. Thus they become Rorschach tests of a kind. Beside each of our 100 photos, we have included a story, meant to amplify and clarify what is being seen, to push the image beyond its boundaries and give greater context. To propel the narrative further still. Thus there is Ruth and Robinson and Rickey and Nolan Ryan and . . . Ryan Howard? The Phillies' lefthanded slugger is no immortal of the game. He is, though, among the many thousands of ballplayers who have stood out by the stands signing autographs before a game, and in Howard's image and in his story, lives something of the whole. Much as the boys on page 196 are hardly the only kids to scale a wall to see a ballgame in the Dominican Republic. You could say they're climbing up at the same time that they're standing in.

There are not pictures of everything of course. Truthfully there aren't very good pictures of *most* things. Were this 100-stop unspooling of baseball's life defined solely by news value, we would have certainly included a photo of Ron Blomberg's first at bat of the day on April 6, 1973, and perhaps of Ted Williams's final at bat of his career, on Sept. 28, 1960. Blomberg came up for the Yankees at Fenway Park as the majors' first designated hitter, forever disrupting the structure and complicating the soul of the game. When Williams came up for the 9,788th time in his singular career, also at Fenway, he hit his 521st home run, a dramatic farewell blast for which he took no bow and gave no acknowledgment to the enraptured home crowd. But the pictures of these particular events are not much to look at. As images, they don't make the grade. Neither does the blurred gray mass depicting Babe Ruth's reputedly called shot in the '32 World Series, a legend with few equals. Even some far more recent events, among them those that have left strong visual impressions through video—the Kirk Gibson home run that won Game 1 of the '88 World Series, for example—didn't yield a photograph with the quality or vibrancy or nuance of a classic.

Inevitably we struck a balance in our selection, so that the strength of the image and the worthiness of the content merged. We added, as lagniappe, salient quotes to bind the message further still. One hundred quotes from 98 people. (Two grand figures are quoted twice.)

Are 100 photographs enough? Enough to tell the story of a sport over 150 years? Enough to tell a story as infinite

———

Have you seen the sweat and dirt that mark the flannel uniform of DiMaggio, rounding first in 1941? Or the lights behind Joe Carter held aloft?

as any reader, any fan would like it to be? No. It's not enough at all. You could do 100 photos of Joe DiMaggio alone. Have you seen the sweat and dirt that marks the flannel uniform of DiMaggio, rounding first in 1941? Or the stadium lights burning bright behind Joe Carter held aloft? Or the hair that whips behind Mone Davis on the mound? We could have done 100 photos of Pete Rose, thrillingly airborne as he is at left, or crashing his way home in the 1970 All-Star Game (the one we chose) or at a podium in 1989, being banished under glare. We could have shown Sandy Koufax in the trainer's room with his left elbow in a bucket of ice, or shown him (as we did) in a moment of triumph, of greatness.

Or maybe 100 photos are enough after all. For within such limits, the infinity. Nine innings. Fifty-four outs. One hundred and sixty-two games. And here 100 photographs to describe a game that has long since slipped its own gentle bounds and has given so many of us moments, memories and, yes, images, we may never forget.

1869
to
1919

Seamless cover National League ball, 1890

Beginnings

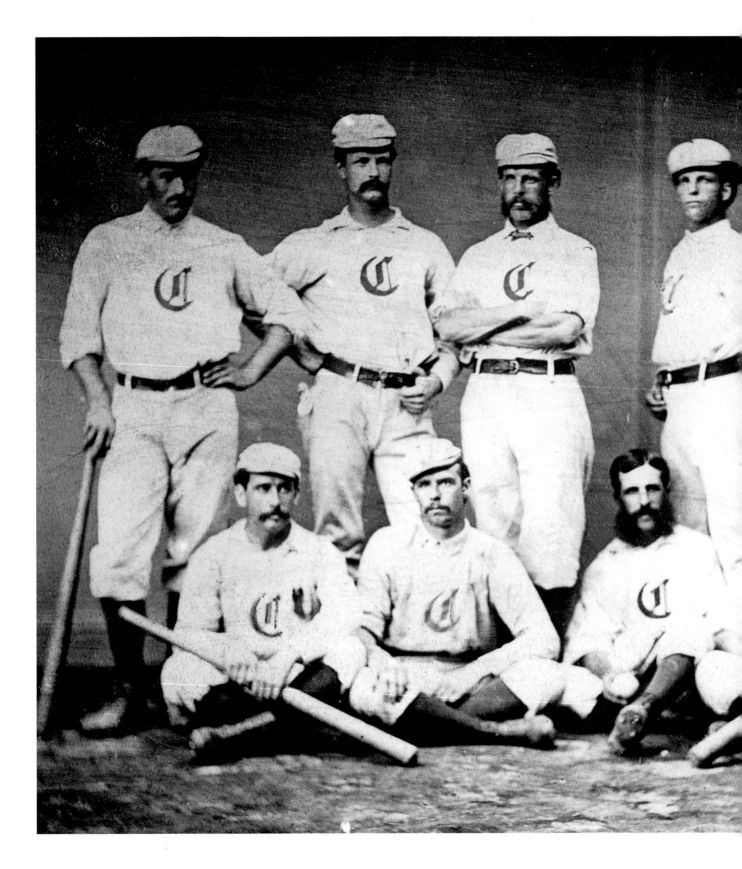

THE ORIGINALS

PHOTO STUDIO, WASHINGTON, D.C. | *June 25, 1869*

WHAT YOU SEE to the left is the true beginning of modern baseball. Back in the day—the really old day, say 1846—teams consisted of locals, who were playing for free. With the '69 Cincinnati Red Stockings, baseball started to become a league of hired ringers who might come from anywhere. These Red Stockings were the first baseball club whose roster was made up entirely of salaried professionals. What's more, those salaries were made public and printed in the newspaper. Before then, if a team was paying a player, it had the decency to keep it quiet. But the Red Stockings let everyone know that player/manager Harry Wright (*top row, middle*) was making $1,200 for the season. His brother George (*no mustache*) was getting $1,400. The Red Stockings' total payroll was $9,300.

They played like moneymakers too. The Red Stockings plowed through their schedule undefeated, going 68-0-1 (some sources count only 57 games, or 65) and knocking off clubs such as the Marion (Ind.) Marions, the St. Louis Unions and the Boston Harvards. The team traveled 12,000 miles, from coast to coast that year. The most controversial game was the tie, against the Troy (N.Y.) Haymakers. It was rumored that tens of thousands of dollars had been bet on the game. After Troy rallied to tie it up, the Haymakers president pulled his team from the field—nominally in protest of an umpire's call. But the perception was that betting interests led to the decision. *The Cincinnati Gazette* ran an editorial railing against the poor behavior of the visitor. It was decidedly unprofessional. And professionalism was on its way to becoming the new standard for baseball.

Photograph by NATIONAL BASEBALL HALL OF FAME LIBRARY

BEGINNING OF THE WORLD

HUNTINGTON AVENUE GROUNDS, BOSTON | *October 1, 1903*

THE FIRST WORLD SERIES was more a peace offering than a battle for supremacy. In 1901 and '02 the National League and the American League had been locked in pitched battle. The NL, formed in 1876, was baseball's top circuit, but in 1901 the American League declared major league ambitions, placing franchises in NL cities and engaging in bidding wars for top players. In '03 the leagues reached a truce and commemorated it with the creation of the World Series. Postseason play between leagues was not unprecedented. There had been such games in the 1880s, and in 1902, the NL champ Pittsburgh Pirates played an exhibition series against an AL All-Star team. This first World Series was a best-of-nine affair, in which the Boston Americans (renamed the Red Sox in '08) beat the Pirates five games to three. Boston's Cy Young threw the first pitch in the inaugural World Series before a crowd of more than 16,000, about three times the average of what Boston drew at home. Young lost that game but won two others while Pittsburgh's Honus Wagner became the first star to lay a postseason egg, batting .222 after leading both leagues with a .355 average. In '04 there was no World Series at all—New York Giants manager John McGraw said his NL champs didn't need to prove themselves against the upstart league—but it resumed in '05, a tectonic step in the development of major league baseball.

Photograph by BETTMANN/GETTY IMAGES

GOOD CHRISTY

SPRING TRAINING | *1906*

IN THE ROUGH and tumble early days of baseball, Christy Mathewson stood tall, in more ways than one. At 6' 1", the pitcher's lofty presence earned him the nickname Big Six. But his character also elevated him above the crowd. A poetry writer and glee club member at Bucknell, where he was junior-class president, Mathewson on the diamond was an exemplar of rectitude—as well as baseball's biggest star of the 1900s. A popular story about Mathewson involved a play at the plate in which the umpire called him safe, but Mathewson confessed that he had been tagged out; when the catcher asked why he did that, Mathewson declared that as a church elder, he was obliged to tell the truth.

The New York Giants righthander was, however, happy to deceive batters, which he did with an array of pitches, including his "fadeaway," a screwball variation that strained his arm so much that he could only throw it a few times a game. Mathewson won 373 games in 17 seasons (that's third all-time), including 37 in 1908. He pitched to a withering 1.14 ERA in '09, one of five times he led the league. He was at his best in the 1905 World Series, when he threw complete-game shutouts in all three of his starts. At age 38, two years removed from the game, Mathewson enlisted in the Army for World War I and became a captain in the Chemical Warfare Service, a unit whose creation was a reaction to the use of chemical weapons in combat. His outfit included baseball luminaries Ty Cobb, George Sisler and Branch Rickey. During a training exercise in France, near the end of the war, Mathewson was accidentally gassed. He soon developed tuberculosis, which plagued him until his death at age 45.

Photograph by NATIONAL BASEBALL HALL OF FAME LIBRARY

> "Learn what pitch you can hit
> good. Then wait for that pitch."
> **—WEE WILLIE KEELER**

A MASTER STROKE

HILLTOP PARK, NEW YORK CITY | *June of 1908*

WEE WILLIE KEELER was one of the earliest sources of a baseball quote for the ages. When a writer for the *Brooklyn Eagle* asked him in 1901 about writing a treatise on his hitting philosophy, the 5' 4" Keeler, who had won two batting titles, replied, "I have already written a treatise, and it reads like this: 'Keep your eye clear and hit 'em where they ain't; that's all.' " His quote, though cheeky in its simplicity, gave real insight into a batting approach that helped him top 200 hits in eight consecutive seasons (while playing in an average of 132 games). Keeler was a master at dropping bunts when infielders were back or hitting high choppers and then racing down the line and beating the throw to first. (The latter technique, popular with Keeler and Orioles teammates such as John McGraw, became known as the Baltimore chop). If the infielders came in, Keeler would loft the ball over their heads. Of his 2,932 career hits, 2,513 were singles. More telling of his batting style and his era: Of his 33 career home runs, 30 were inside the park. His feats set standards that proved difficult to top. His 45-game hitting streak over the 1896–1897 seasons was exceeded by Joe DiMaggio in 1941, but remains the official National League mark—Pete Rose came within one game of it in '78. Keeler's name surfaced again when Ichiro Suzuki broke his record of singles in a season (206 in 1898) in 2004, and then exceeded Keeler's mark for consecutive 200-hit seasons in '09. As one of the smallest players ever, Wee Willie swung a very short but quite heavy bat (30 inches, 46 ounces). With it he left a giant impression.

Photograph by BAIN COLLECTION/LIBRARY OF CONGRESS

THE PITCHER, THE NAMESAKE

HUNTINGTON AVENUE GROUNDS, BOSTON | *July 23, 1908*

DENTON TRUE YOUNG'S formal education stopped at grade six so he could work on the family farm in Ohio. For youthful diversion, he would hunt squirrels by throwing stones at them. Whenever he could he would play baseball, and he became good enough to earn a buck a game in semipro ball. It was during a tryout with the Canton team that he was given his nickname. Young was called upon to pitch with a wooden grandstand as the only backstop, and afterward the grandstand was so beat up that, an onlooker observed, it looked as if it had been battered by a cyclone. From Canton, Cy Young quickly advanced to the big leagues with the Cleveland Spiders and began to pile up more wins (511) than any pitcher in history. This was a different time, to be sure. As a rookie he pitched both ends of a doubleheader, winning each game. But Young had traits valued in any era. For 14 seasons he had the lowest walk rate in baseball. Despite no exercise routine beyond his farmwork, he had extraordinary durability. He pitched until age 44 and became baseball's all-time leader in innings pitched while throwing a record 749 complete games. Young was also remarkably grounded. (On at least two occasions he filled in for an umpire who had failed to show up for the game.) When he was done with baseball, he went back to the farm. He died in 1955, at age 88, and the next year baseball began honoring its best pitchers with the annual Cy Young Award.

Photograph by BAIN COLLECTION/LIBRARY OF CONGRESS

> "It has never been a pleasant subject for me to discuss. For years while I continued to play, it haunted me and kept me in constant fear of, 'What can happen to me now?'"
> —FRED MERKLE

THE BONER AT COOGAN'S BLUFF

POLO GROUNDS, NEW YORK CITY | *October 8, 1908*

BASEBALL INSTITUTED VIDEO review in 2008, exactly 100 years after the Merkle Boner game—a day when it really would have come in handy. Two key elements of the famed play were in dispute, in a game that altered the outcome of the 1908 season. The matchup between the Cubs and the Giants took place at the funky, early version of the Polo Grounds. Fans had began gathering to watch the Giants from the overlook beyond the outfield (Coogan's Bluff) since the 1890s. The game was tied in the bottom of the ninth, and New York had runners on first and third. A hit to the outfield drove in the runner from third, apparently winning the game for the Giants. But Cubs infielder Johnny Evers argued that 19-year-old rookie Fred Merkle, the runner on first base, had left the field without ever touching second—having peeled off toward the clubhouse, as players often did in those days, to avoid fans coming onto the diamond. Evers got his hands on the ball (or *a* ball) and touched second to force out Merkle. The Giants argued that Merkle had returned to second base in time and that furthermore, Evers never received the actual ball but a substitute (in some accounts, a fan on the field threw the game ball into the stands). Still, the umpire called Merkle out and then suspended the game without a final result due to darkness. When the teams ended the season tied for first, the game was replayed in its entirety (the fans at right are watching the pennant-deciding playoff). Chicago won 4–2, took the National League pennant and went on to win the '08 World Series, their last for 108 years. Fred Merkle played in five World Series, losing all five, over 14 more seasons in the majors.

Photograph by TRANSCENDENTAL GRAPHICS/GETTY IMAGES

> "We all used to collect baseball cards that came with bubble gum. You could never get the smell of gum off your cards, but you kept your Yankees cards pristine."
> —**PENNY MARSHALL,** ACTRESS AND FILM DIRECTOR

MOST VALUABLE

NORTH CAROLINA, BY WAY OF PITTSBURGH | *Issued 1909*

TRADING CARDS HAVE long been intertwined in America's love affair with baseball. On these rectangular pieces of cardboard, stars such as Joe DiMaggio, Hank Aaron and Mike Schmidt became not just players kids rooted and cheered for, but also ones they flipped and scaled and traded for. Young fans kept shoeboxes full of their idols, photos on the front and stats on the back, in their bedrooms. Collectors bought and sold the cards, angling for bargains, at conventions and fairs. Baseball cards are still very much around today of course, but their heyday ran from the 1950s to the '90s, when packs of cards—found at your local newsstand or deli or candy shop—came with a dusty piece of pink bubble gum. That was also a time frame that produced some of the most valuable and talked-about cards: The '52 Mantle, the '55 Clemente, the '63 Rose and others. Initially though, the cards were produced and distributed by tobacco companies, and from that early era comes the most valuable of them all.

In 1909 Honus Wagner, the Pirates' shortstop, asked the Durham, N.C.–based American Tobacco Company to stop including his card with their products. Wagner was known to smoke cigars and chew tobacco, but he loathed cigarettes. Some speculated he may have wanted more money for the use of his image. Whatever the reason, Wagner's card, numbered T206, was pulled after only about 200 reached the public. About 60 are believed to exist today. The scarcity, combined with the card's simple beauty and Wagner's Hall of Fame status, have proved an irresistible combination for collectors. In October 2016 a well-preserved version of the T206 was sold at auction for $3.12 million, a trading-card record, breaking the $2.8 million paid for another version of the Wagner card.

Photograph by KATHY WILLENS/AP/SHUTTERSTOCK

WAGNER, PITTSBURG

A PRIMAL FORCE

HILLTOP PARK, NEW YORK CITY | *July 23, 1910*

THANKS IN PART to the attention paid to Pete Rose's 1980s pursuit of his all-time hits record, fans associate Ty Cobb with his plate heroics. That makes sense: His career batting average of .366 is the best ever—by a lot. He led the league in hitting 12 times. But in his day Cobb was at least as feared for what he did after he got on base. He stole 897 bases, the most by a 20th century player besides Rickey Henderson and Lou Brock, and he ran in all situations with a withering aggression. Pittsburgh's Max Carey, another top base stealer of this time, said of Cobb, "His idea was not only to get the extra bases but to destroy the morale of the pitcher, the catcher, the entire infield." Cobb, who once cut Frank "Home Run" Baker's forearm on a slide into third, is alleged to have sharpened the spikes on his cleats. A former Tigers batboy named Jimmy Lanier said in a 2010 interview that he cleaned Cobb's spikes and never saw anything amiss, adding, "I believe he used the 'sharpening the spikes' rumor as an advantage, making the opposing players fearful of getting cut trying to tag him when he slid into a base." Cobb's game was designed to dominate a Dead Ball era whose passing he lamented when the long ball came to rule the sport. But when baseball chose its inaugural Hall of Fame class in 1936, Cobb earned the highest percentage of votes, finishing ahead of even Babe Ruth. Cobb had the respect, and fear, of his peers.

Photograph by CHARLES M. CONLON
SPORTING NEWS ARCHIVE/GETTY IMAGES

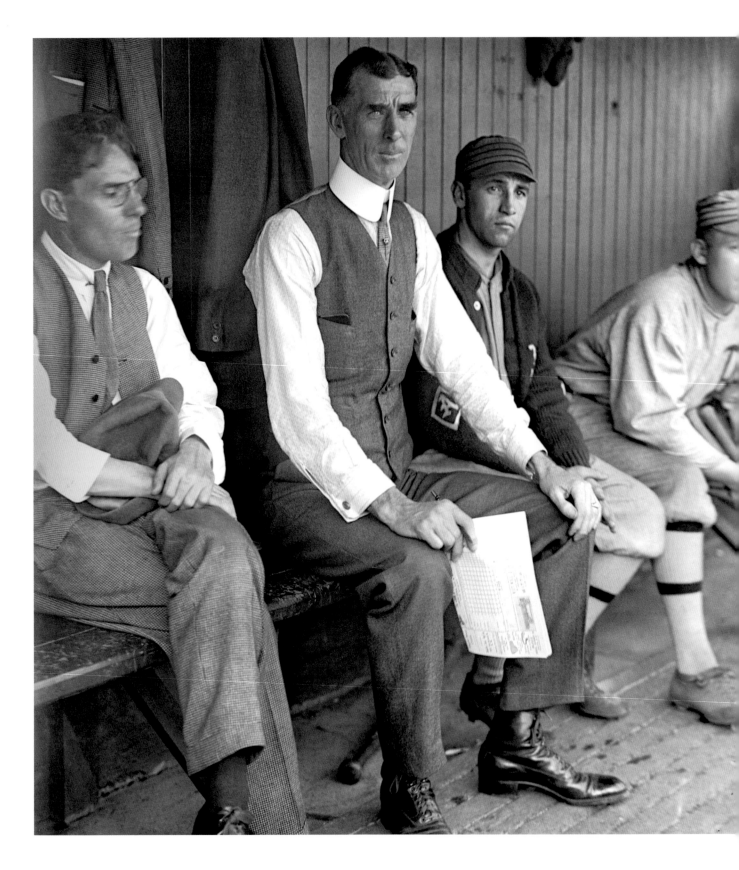

A HALF CENTURY OF CLASS

GRIFFITH STADIUM, WASHINGTON, D.C. | *June of 1913*

AS A PLAYER in the late 1800s Connie Mack could be a bit of a sneak. A catcher, he'd make a clucking noise to trick the umpire into thinking Mack had caught a foul tip, which in those days meant the batter was out. He also would disturb hitters by delivering up a stream of chatter that, while lighter on curse words than those of other catchers, sought to undermine their confidence. In 1901 Mack, 38, became manager (and treasurer and part-owner) of the fledgling Philadelphia Athletics. He held that manager's job for 50—yes, 50—years. Players were born, had full careers and retired while Mack remained a constant in the A's dugout, always dressed in a suit and with scorecard in hand. As manager his words were notably supportive. He didn't bark at his players in public, favoring private instruction over public criticism. His players called him Mr. Mack.

His A's teams won nine pennants and five World Series, but also endured plenty of last-place finishes. Mack's overall managerial record (which includes a few pre-A's seasons leading the Pittsburgh Pirates) finished up at 3,731–3,948. He has nearly 1,000 more wins, and 1,600 more losses than any other manager in history. Those losing seasons often came partly because Mack was under financial pressure and had to jettison the stars that had won him the championships—names such as Eddie Collins, "Home Run" Baker, Al Simmons, Mickey Cochrane, Lefty Grove and Jimmie Foxx. Losing also led Mack to suffer a nervous breakdown in '21, after which he vowed, "I told myself after that, that I'd never let it happen again. I'd always be ready to take the bad with the good." So he endured, having the occasional dugout nap toward the end of his career, which came in 1950, when he was 87 years old. By then everyone in the game was calling him Mr. Mack. Baseball will never have a grander old man.

Photograph by HARRIS & EWING COLLECTION/ LIBRARY OF CONGRESS

FAST AND EASY

POLO GROUNDS, NEW YORK CITY | *April 12, 1916*

HIS PITCHING MOTION WAS, like the man himself, quiet. Walter Johnson's daughter once said that whenever her father, raised on a Kansas farm, had something to say, she listened, because he spoke so rarely that she knew it had to be important. On the mound, Johnson's body had similar economy. His kick was minimal. His arm stayed below shoulder height and came across his body with little snap at the elbow or wrist. And yet the fastballs that whistled across the plate earned him the nickname The Big Train. He became the first of baseball's famous fastballers, known as the hardest thrower in the game and an inspiration to measure the speed of pitches. In 1914, Johnson's fastball was pitted in a 60-foot race against a motorcycle. The ball speed was measured at 99.7 miles an hour.

His pitching style had to have been easy on the shoulder, given the workload he managed. With the Washington Senators in 1908, over Labor Day weekend, Johnson started three games in four days against the Yankees and shut them out each time, surrendering a total of 12 hits. In '18 he threw an 18-inning, 1–0 win over the White Sox, hardly an unusual result as the Senators could be stingy with run support. (He pitched in a record 64 1–0 games, winning 38 and losing 26.) Johnson's 5,914⅓ innings pitched are third all-time, and he has other mind-boggling numbers: 417 wins, 531 complete games, 110 shutouts, a 1913 season in which he went 36–7 with a 1.14 ERA. When Johnson was signed from semipro ball, he had so little confidence that he asked that his Senators contract include a guaranteed return train ticket home. It was not a ticket he would need.

Photograph by BETTMANN/GETTY IMAGES

1920 to 1947

Lou Gehrig's glove, 1930

From Ruth to Robinson

SAY IT AIN'T SO, JOE

ROAD GAME | *1920*

JOE JACKSON WAS both an exceptional player and a thrilling one: His .356 career average is the third-highest ever, and he led the league in triples three times. He had a memorable nickname, although he hated being called Shoeless, because he had only played once in his stocking feet, in the minors, because his shoes weren't broken in. Still, the nickname played into his common-man appeal. Jackson was from South Carolina, illiterate, and during his first season he left the Philadelphia A's after three games because he was homesick. The other thing about Shoeless Joe is that he made a bad decision. He and seven White Sox teammates were accused of conspiring to throw the 1919 World Series, a best-of-nine series that the Cincinnati Reds won in eight. A Chicago jury acquitted the players, but Jackson and all participants in the so-called Black Sox scandal were banished from the game by new commissioner Kenesaw Mountain Landis in 1921—about 10 months after Jackson, 33, finished the '20 season with a .382 batting average.

Over the years movements have risen to elect Jackson (who died in '51) into the Baseball Hall of Fame. His advocates point to his .375 average in that World Series and his perfect record in the field. Yet in pretrial grand jury testimony Jackson acknowledged that he had been in on a fix. "Q: Did anybody pay you any money to help throw that series in favor of Cincinnati? A: They did. Q: How much did they pay? A: They promised me $20,000 and paid me five." Jackson also added, "We went ahead and threw the second game."

Even banned from the game Jackson had been fully eligible for induction into the Hall of Fame for the first 55 years of its existence. He received some votes but never nearly enough to get in. Then in 1991 the Hall's board, determined to deprive baseball writers of the opportunity to vote on Pete Rose, who was banned for gambling, passed a rule making anyone on baseball's ineligible list also ineligible for the Hall. That rule, along with his admission of throwing a World Series game means that Shoeless Joe and his .356 average will forever be on the outside, looking in.

Photograph by CORBIS/GETTY IMAGES

HOT DOGS HERE!

EBBETS FIELD, BROOKLYN, N.Y. | *October 6, 1920*

THE HOT DOG was baptized in a baseball park. Sausages were sold at St. Louis Browns games as far back as the 1890s and then, in 1900, as legend has it, cartoonist Tad Dorgan was at the Polo Grounds on a cold day in New York and saw "red-hot dachshund sausages" being sold. He dubbed the sausages "hot dogs," and a German delicacy became an American tradition. With that, the menu for U.S. spectator sports had been set by baseball—before the country's other sports leagues had even formed. Baseball, with its mid-inning breaks and bite-sized pauses between batters, is built for hot dog consumption. The hot dog, boiled or grilled, is easy to hold, easy to pass down the row, easy to customize with mustard and relish. The hot dog has also proven amazingly adaptable as American tastes have matured and the game has spread. The variations of hot dog available at big league ballparks are, frankly, astounding. Arizona has the Asada Dog (the main event is supplemented by queso blanco, carne asada, pico de gallo and guacamole), Baltimore has the Crab Mac n Cheese dog and Cincinnati has the Skyline chili coney. Milwaukee's Wisconsin dog is topped with bacon and beer jam sauerkraut and at Rangers' games in Texas you can get a decidely decadent Dilly Dog, in which a dill pickle is cored out, stuffed with a hot dog, then battered and fried. These parks, like all of the others in the majors and the minors, also offer the basic dog, for those who like it the way it used to be.

Photograph by BAIN COLLECTION/LIBRARY OF CONGRESS

"A Presidential candidate, selecting Times Square as an appropriate place for an open-air address, could not have attracted more people."
—**THE NEW YORK TIMES** ON THE ASSEMBLED CROWD FOR THE 1920 WORLD SERIES

TUNING IN

TIMES SQUARE, NEW YORK CITY | *October 12, 1920*

THESE PEOPLE GATHERED in Times Square are not waiting for the ball to drop—or at least, not that kind of ball. These fans came for updates on the World Series. It was not until 1921 that baseball began to be broadcast on the radio and before then crowds would gather in public squares for updates on the action, delivered by telegraph and then translated to a scoreboard, showing runners on the base paths, with counters for balls and strikes and runs and outs. The display was not unlike what fans see today when they are following a game in isolation on their computer or phone. Back then an Atlanta opera house took the pantomime to an amusing extreme, illustrating the action on the field with uniformed human beings moving around their stage. But the scoreboards were more typical. In this photo thousands waited for updates on Game 7 of the '20 World Series between the Brooklyn Robins (then one of the franchise nicknames, along with Dodgers) against the Cleveland Indians. The scoreboard was outside the Times Tower on Broadway, and the size of the crowd shows the growing fascination that baseball was having on the American public. A report in the *New York Times* described fans showing up well before the first pitch was thrown, and yelling managerial advice at the scoreboards. The piece said that people seemed to be as worked up as if they were at the ballpark. The Indians won the game and took the best-of-nine series five games to two.

Photograph by PHILIPP KESTER/ULLSTEIN BILD/GETTY IMAGES

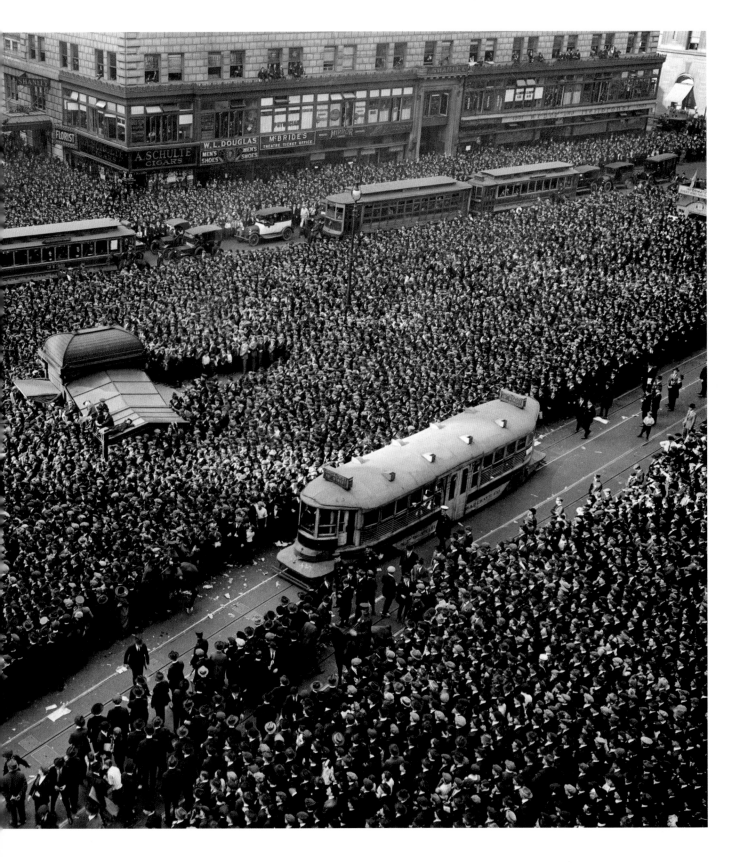

> "Baseball is something more than a game to an American boy; it is his training field for life's work. Destroy his faith in its squareness and honesty and you have destroyed something more; you have planted suspicion of all things in his heart."
> —**KENESAW MOUNTAIN LANDIS**

THE FIRST COMMISSIONER

POLO GROUNDS, NEW YORK CITY | *June 10, 1922*

BASEBALL WAS AT a low point, the integrity of the game having been sullied by the Black Sox scandal in which members of the Chicago White Sox conspired to throw the 1919 World Series. Gambling had been close to the game in its earlier years, but this was more ominous. Fans were upset and baseball team owners were concerned—which is why in November of 1920 they hired Judge Kenesaw Mountain Landis as the first commissioner of baseball, or of any sport. Landis, a federal judge, had a reputation for handing out harsh sentences. Many of his rulings were overturned on appeal, but the hard-line reputation was a public relations plus. Also, Landis was a baseball fan, and owners liked the way he had handled a '15 antitrust case against them that resulted in a favorable outcome. As commissioner, Landis immediately banned for life the eight White Sox players accused of throwing the Series. That was just the start. In '22

he dropped the hammer on the game's biggest star, Babe Ruth, suspending him for 40 games for offseason barnstorming. That year Landis also permanently banned Giants pitcher Phil Douglas after Douglas suggested he was going to quit to spite his team.

During his reign, which lasted until 1944, Landis banned 18 people for life, the last coming in '43, when Phillies owner William D. Cox was found to have bet on games. Cox had become an owner after a potential sale of the franchise to Bill Veeck did not materialize. Veeck claimed that an agreement was in place until he told the league of his intention to stock the team with Negro leagues stars. Landis's shortsightedness on integration may have been his great shortcoming. His firmness against gambling in baseball was his great strength.

Photograph by NATIONAL BASEBALL HALL OF FAME LIBRARY/GETTY IMAGES

THE BABE

SPORTSMAN'S PARK, ST. LOUIS | *October 6, 1926*

BABE RUTH DIDN'T break a mold so much as create one. He began his career at the end of a Dead Ball era, when managers emphasized baserunning and defense, and the sacrifice bunt was a significant offensive weapon. But rules changes—including the banning of the spitball in 1920 and enforcement of regulations against other doctored pitches—set the stage for a new kind of offensive star, and Ruth showed baseball the power of swinging for the fences.

He began his career in 1914 as a mighty lefthanded pitcher with the Red Sox, going 67–34 with a 2.07 ERA over his first four seasons. But Ruth soon saw that he would be better off concentrating his energies at the plate. In '19 he hit 29 home runs, then a single-season record. That offseason Boston sold his contract to the Yankees for $100,000. In the first year in his new home Ruth hit an astonishing 54 home runs, more than the totals of every other team in the league but one. The original "Ruthian" blasts elevated this former Baltimore street urchin with the moon-shaped face into the biggest star sports had ever known—given to feats such as hitting three home runs in a single World Series game, which he is in the process of doing in the photo at right. Ruth was a hot-dog eating, whiskey-drinking, showgirl-dating, orphan-aiding, shot-calling, management-sassing, big-money-earning Sultan of Swat. And in the years following the 1919 Black Sox scandal, when many baseball fans were disillusioned or disenchanted, Ruth was a player to enchant and to believe in. He set home run records for a single season (60 in '27) and a career (714) that stood for decades, and to this day he holds the career mark in slugging percentage and OPS. Ruth was the best.

Photograph by BETTMANN/GETTY IMAGES

THE MIDSUMMER CLASSIC

COMISKEY PARK, CHICAGO | *July 6, 1933*

THE WORLD'S FAIR came to Chicago in 1933, featuring such modern wonders as an animatronic King Kong and the "towering skyride," a suspended cable-car system that promised a future of urban travel through the air. *Chicago Tribune* sports editor Arch Ward helped push the idea that his city, already honoring the progress of the modern world, should celebrate America's pastime by gathering baseball's best players on one field. The presidents of the American and National Leagues agreed, and the first major league All-Star game in any sport was born. The game, held at Comiskey Park, sold out its 47,595 seats in two days. The starting players, were chosen by fan voting, and late-career Babe Ruth delivered a two-run home run that propelled the American League to a 4–2 win. The exhibition had been proposed as a one-off, but it immediately became the annual midsummer entertainment that it remains to this day.

The All-Star Game was especially compelling in an age when players changed teams infrequently and there was no interleague play; the game offered potentially once-in-a-lifetime clashes of the titans. No one delivered on that stage like New York Giants lefty Carl Hubbell (shown here on the dugout steps with Lefty Grove, with Ruth in back and to the right). In the 1934 edition of the game, Hubbell struck out, in order, five future Hall of Famers: Ruth, Lou Gehrig, Jimmie Foxx, Al Simmons and Joe Cronin. The '34 game took place at the Polo Grounds, and New York didn't have any World's Fair going on, but what Hubbell accomplished with his befuddling screwball was truly an exhibition of wonder.

Photograph by BETTMANN/GETTY IMAGES

THE CATCHER WAS A SPY

GRIFFITH STADIUM, WASHINGTON, D.C. | *September 6, 1933*

MOE BERG GRADUATED from Princeton in 1923—with a B.A., magna cum laude in modern languages. He had one job offer to teach romance languages at the school and another to play for the Brooklyn Dodgers. He chose baseball and played 15 seasons for five teams, largely as a backup catcher. But his life beyond baseball was extraordinary. One offseason he studied at the Sorbonne in Paris. During others he attended Columbia Law School, passed the bar and worked on Wall Street. When baseball sent an All-Star team to tour Japan in 1934, they invited Berg because he could converse with his hosts in Japanese. In Tokyo on that trip Berg skipped a game one day and bluffed his way into a hospital on the pretext of seeing a patient. Once admitted, he found his way to the roof (this was one of the city's tallest buildings) and, with a camera he had hidden, filmed the Tokyo cityscape. In '42 that footage was useful to American bombers in their air attacks on Tokyo. During World War II, Berg, retired from baseball, was employed by the Office of Strategic Services, the precursor to the CIA, and he was sent to Europe to befriend the physicists suspected of helping Germany develop nuclear weapons. He was also given orders to assassinate German atomic scientist Werner Heisenberg if he was deemed dangerous. After sitting through a lecture given by the scientist in Zurich, concealed pistol at hand, and later dining with Heisenberg, Berg deduced that Germany was far from having nuclear capabilities. All this from a career .243 hitter who would pass slow afternoons in the bullpen with stories from his travels. Some teammates wondered, What is he even doing here? In Nicholas Dawidoff's book *The Catcher Was a Spy*, Berg's brother explained Moe's years in baseball by saying, "All it ever did was make him happy."

Photograph by STANLEY WESTON ARCHIVE/GETTY IMAGES

BRIGHT IDEA

CROSLEY FIELD, CINCINNATI | *May 24, 1935*

THERE WAS A time, a long time in fact, when major league baseball games could be called on account of darkness, prey to the same forces that would send kids off the sandlot and back inside on a summer night. The beginning of the end of that era came in 1935, when Reds general manager Larry MacPhail, pressed by owner Powel Crosley Jr. to increase attendance, decided to try night baseball. Night games had already been played at minor league parks and in Negro leagues games, but with rough setups that provided only patchy illumination. MacPhail's Reds invested $50,000 at Crosley Field to build eight light towers festooned with 632 1,500-watt bulbs. When the Reds held their first night game on May 24, 1935 *(pictured at left)*, President Franklin Delano Roosevelt joined in the theater of the moment by hitting a telegraph key from Washington, D.C., that signaled when to flip the switch that turned on the stadium lights. In that first game the Reds beat the Phillies 2–1. Afterward Reds infielder Billy Myers said the major league version of night baseball was much better, commenting, "In the minor leagues, you couldn't see the outfielders." Fan opinion was clear. That first season, in seven games the Reds averaged 18,620 for night games, compared to 4,607 for day games. Soon other teams followed, and by '48 the majority of teams and the majority of games were being played at night. The last holdouts were the Chicago Cubs, whose owner, Philip K. Wrigley, resisted the switch to night baseball. But Wrigley died in '77, and the less idiosyncratic Tribune Company brought the team. In 1988 lights came to Wrigley. All of MLB was illuminated.

Photograph by SCHENECTADY MUSEUM/HALL OF ELECTRICAL HISTORY FOUNDATION/CORBIS/GETTY IMAGES

> "I played with Willie Mays and against Hank Aaron. They were tremendous players, but they were no Josh Gibson."
> —**MONTE IRVIN**, NEGRO LEAGUES AND MLB HALL OF FAME OUTFIELDER

ELITE, UNDER ANY CONDITIONS

GREENLEE FIELD, PITTSBURGH | *1936*

THE PITTSBURGH CRAWFORDS of the mid-1930s were the Negro leagues' answer to the New York Yankees, winning three league championships in a four-year span. This stocked team featured Josh Gibson, a prodigious slugger known as the black Babe Ruth, and Cool Papa Bell, who was so fast, teammate Satchel Paige quipped, that he could flip the light switch and be in bed before the room was dark. The player-manager Oscar Charleston was reminiscent of Ty Cobb at the plate and made dazzling catches in centerfield, and team captain Judy Johnson was a wizard at third.

So, in one sense the Crawfords were a dream team, although the bus in this photo gives a sense of the economic disparity between the Negro leagues and the majors. (The Yankees traveled on Pullman trains with dining cars.) The Negro leagues, which began in 1920, were a vibrant force in baseball, until after the time that Jackie Robinson jumped from the Kansas City Monarchs for the Brooklyn Dodgers organization in '46. Robinson's success created opportunity for other players who followed, but also ultimately led to the Negro leagues' demise. Even the African-American press, which had provided the most regular coverage of Negro leagues games, became more interested in following its former stars in the bigs. In '71 the Baseball Hall of Fame inducted Paige, the first such honor bestowed on a player whose career had been spent mostly in the Negro leagues. Paige was soon followed into the Hall by those Crawfords teammates Gibson, Bell, Johnson and Charleston—a recognition of the excellence consigned to this bus.

Photograph by NATIONAL BASEBALL HALL OF FAME LIBRARY

WHAT A GAS

EBBETS FIELD, BROOKLYN, N.Y. | *1937*

THEY WERE A TEAM for their time. The popularity of the Gashouse Gang blossomed as America suffered through the deep middle of the Great Depression. The Cardinals' organization then was one of the cheapest in baseball, and fans embraced their players with their rowdy attitudes and dirty uniforms, as another group of guys getting by on less than they should. The team, frequent contenders, was stocked with players from poor backgrounds who took the field with an aggressive cockiness. Manager Frankie Frisch was notoriously pugnacious. The shortstop was Leo "the Lip" Durocher. Ace pitcher Dizzy Dean, discovered by a scout in a Texas Army base game, brought the heat in interviews as well as on the mound. Before their 1934 World-Series-winning season he boasted that he would win 20 to 25 games, and his brother Daffy 18 to 20. (Dizzy's guess was a little low: He won 30, Daffy 19.) Hall of Famer Joe "Ducky" Medwick, a Triple Crown winner, was a quick wit too. After being pelted by garbage by Detroit fans in that '34 World Series following an on-field scuffle, he quipped "I knew why [Tigers fans] threw that garbage at me. What I don't understand is why they brought it to the park in the first place." In this photo are other merry-making members of the gang, specifically the Mudcat Band who played real gigs with real instruments (at games and on radio shows and during offseason tours) as well as bats: Bob "Lefty" Weiland, Lon Warneke, Frenchy Bordagaray, Bill "Fiddler" McGee and Pepper Martin. Along with being the bandleader, Martin was a four-time All-Star who once, on a road trip to Philadelphia, went to a fancy hotel dressed as a fireman and set off smoke bombs to the horror of a restaurant full of lunching ladies. These guys weren't afraid to mess around.

Photograph by IRVING HABERMAN/IH IMAGES/GETTY IMAGES

THE ONE PERCENT

COOPERSTOWN, NEW YORK | *June 12, 1939*

THERE HAD NEVER been a hall of fame for any sport until baseball created one. In 1936, before the actual hall and its accompanying museum were built, five players were chosen, by the Baseball Writers' Association of America, for the inaugural class (Ty Cobb, Walter Johnson, Christy Mathewson, Babe Ruth and Honus Wagner). Three years later, 20 more had been inducted, some living and some dead, and the physical Hall and its accompanying museum were ready to open in Cooperstown. Baseball decided to make an event of the building dedication and the 11 living Hall of Famers were summoned. Though no one knew how many fans would be attracted to baseball's act of self-celebration, the streets of Cooperstown were clogged, full of baseball lovers who wanted to breathe the same air as their heroes. In the picture are *(front row, left to right)* Eddie Collins, Ruth, Connie Mack and Cy Young; and *(back row)* Wagner, Grover Cleveland Alexander, Tris Speaker, Nap Lajoie, George Sisler and Johnson. Cobb arrived late. The inductee speeches were brief, but Collins captured the feeling of the gathering when he remarked, "This is about the proudest day of my life, to be able to rub elbows with the players that are here today. I feel that, why, I'd be glad to be the batboy for such a team as this." By now there are 323 people who've been elected to the Hall of Fame, among them 226 former major leaguers, about one of every 100 who have ever played the game.

Photograph by NATIONAL BASEBALL HALL OF FAME LIBRARY

LUCKIEST MAN

YANKEE STADIUM, BRONX, N.Y. | *July 4, 1939*

HE WAS BROAD and powerful, and he played every day. And oh, how Lou Gehrig played! Over an extraordinary 11-year peak the great Yankee averaged *an RBI per game*, leading the league five times. He won two MVP awards and in six other seasons finished in the top five in the vote. But in 1939, his 17th season, the Iron Horse was breaking down. The ball came weakly off his bat and in the field, at first base, he could hardly maneuver. On May 2, soon after a play in which he struggled to make it to the bag on a ground ball, Gehrig pulled himself from the lineup, ending his streak of 2,130 games played—and his career. He was found to have amyotrophic lateral sclerosis (now known as Lou Gehrig's disease), and his teammates, heartsick, wanted to pay tribute. The initial plan for a modest clubhouse gathering ballooned into a public ceremony at Yankee Stadium, on July 4, in front of 62,000 fans between games of doubleheader. Well-wishers made speeches and presented gifts—candlesticks, a fruit bowl, a fishing rod. After accepting all these Gehrig was ready to disappear into the clubhouse when, with the crowd chanting, "We Want Lou!" Yankees manager Joe McCarthy urged him to say a few words into the microphone. The taciturn player did so reluctantly, and his words were for the ages. "For the past two weeks, you've been reading about a bad break I got. Yet today I consider myself the luckiest man on the face of the earth." At the time Gehrig still believed he could beat ALS, but people knew he was seriously ill. *Washington Post* columnist Shirley Povich, covering the tribute, wrote, "I saw strong men weep this afternoon." Gehrig died on June 2, 1941.

Photograph by BETTMANN/GETTY IMAGES

BEANED

EBBETS FIELD, BROOKLYN, N.Y. | *June 18, 1940*

CONSEQUENCES CAN BE dire when a batter is struck by a pitch. Mickey Cochrane and Kirby Puckett are Hall of Famers whose careers were shortened by beanballs. Boston's Tony Conigliaro became the youngest player to hit 100 home runs but was never the same after a 1967 pitch hit him in the head and left him with blurred vision. In 1920 Cleveland Indians shortstop Ray Chapman was killed by a pitch.

The man in the photo to the left is Joe Medwick, the 1937 Triple Crown winner and an eventual Hall of Famer, who is out cold on the field after what may or may not have been a purposeful beanball. Medwick, a career Cardinal, had been traded to the Dodgers six days earlier and was facing his former team. The story goes that before the game St. Louis's starting pitcher Bob Bowman was in an elevator with Medwick and Brooklyn's player/manager, Leo Durocher, and the impromptu reunion led to a spat during which Bowman said, "I'll take care of both of you." Whether he was suggesting he would unleash a beanball or merely vowing to pitch effectively is a matter of dispute. Whatever was meant, in the first inning Medwick, batting fourth, faced Bowman, who had already allowed two runs. Bowman threw a fastball that struck Medwick in the head. He was taken to the hospital with a concussion. Medwick came back four days later, and would go on to play until 1948. As others can testify, it could have been worse. But the Medwick moment mattered because in '41, partly due to this incident, his Dodgers became the first team to wear batting helmets. It wasn't until 1971 that baseball mandated that all batters wear helmets, with an ear flap requirement added in '83.

Photograph by THE NEW YORK TIMES/REDUX

JOLTIN' JOE

GRIFFITH STADIUM, WASHINGTON, D.C. | *June 29, 1941*

IT WAS SAID that if you wanted to see how baseball is meant to be played, watch Joe DiMaggio round a base—he did it with such intensity and efficiency. That partly explains why even as a player not associated firstly with speed, he accumulated a surprising number of triples. Similarly, he covered tremendous ground in the outfield, in large part because he knew how to position himself and get a jump and angle on the ball, so he made the catches look easy. At the plate he was rarely fooled: The three-time American League MVP entered his final season, 1951, with more career home runs than strikeouts. Ted Williams called DiMaggio "the greatest all-around player I ever saw. His career cannot be summed up in numbers and awards. It might sound corny, but he had a profound and lasting impact on the country." Indeed, DiMaggio's grace and bearing on the field became the stuff that slipped the bounds of the game. Ernest Hemingway wrote in DiMaggio as a figure of inspiration in *The Old Man and the Sea*. Paul Simon's 1968 lyric "Where have you gone, Joe DiMaggio?/A nation turns its lonely eyes to you" is among the most enduring in popular music. And never was the nation more transfixed than during DiMaggio's astounding 56-game hitting streak, in '41, which captured the country's imagination, a daily dose of news and excitement amid the uncertainty of World War II. DiMaggio, like many others, enlisted and gave three prime seasons to military service. After baseball, DiMaggio married actress Marilyn Monroe, who herself was mythologized into an icon. DiMaggio was no quipster but his most famous bon mot was spoken to her. After Monroe returned from entertaining troops during the Korean War, she said, "Joe, you've never heard such cheering." He replied simply, "Yes, I have."

Photograph by CORBIS/GETTY IMAGES

BASEBALL AND THE WAR

WASHINGTON, D.C. | *February 2, 1942*

FROM 1938 THROUGH 1940 Hank Greenberg hit 132 home runs for the Detroit Tigers, the most of anyone in baseball. And then on May 7, 1941, just 19 games into the year, and a day after hitting two homers in a farewell appearance, he was inducted into the Army, the first star player to join the service. He was discharged from on Dec. 5 when all draftees 28 and older (he was 30) were dismissed. But two days later Japan attacked Pearl Harbor, and Greenberg reenlisted, this time with the Army Air Corps for a stint that lasted until June 1945. His 47 months in the service was the longest tenure of any ballplayer. While baseball continued during World War II, more than 500 players served. Bob Feller also enlisted after Pearl Harbor, and the Cleveland pitcher served as a petty officer on the USS *Alabama*. Joe DiMaggio was in the Navy too, and Stan Musial was in the Army. They played baseball for service teams and helped raise money with exhibitions. Ted Williams received a deferment because his mother was dependent on him, but he was mocked by fans and in the press, and then enlisted in the Navy reserves in '42, learning the fighter pilot skills that he would eventually use in 39 combat missions during the Korean War. Warren Spahn and Hoyt Wilhelm earned Purple Hearts in Europe before going on to Hall of Fame careers. Two players died in service, Washington centerfielder Elmer Gedeon and Philadelphia Athletics catcher Harry O'Neill. Greenberg, initially stationed Stateside as a physical fitness officer, requested a transfer overseas and served as an administrator in India and China. He returned to the U.S., and said "I guess I was just lucky to come back in one piece." His first game back in Detroit, on July 1, 1945, he hit a home run.

Photograph by U.S. ARMY/AP/SHUTTERSTOCK

> "A man has to have goals—for a day, for a lifetime—and that was mine, to have people say, 'There goes Ted Williams, the greatest hitter who ever lived.'"
> —TED WILLIAMS

THE SPLENDID SPLINTER

FENWAY PARK, BOSTON | *April 15, 1947*

TED WILLIAMS WAS the last player to hit .400, and the way he achieved the mark in 1941 hints at his special place in baseball lore. Williams had been well above .400 for most of the season, but in the final week the Boston leftfielder had a few subpar games and came into the season-ending double header in Philadelphia with an average of .39955. Had Williams sat out, he would finished with an official .400 average by virtue of rounding up, but he declared to *The Sporting News*, "I want to have more than my toenails on the line." Williams went 4 for 5 in the first game, and then 2 for 3 in the nightcap before the game was called for darkness. Williams final average: a righteous .406.

This was a man with strong ideas about the correct way to do things. He took his bats to the post office and asked clerks to place them on a scale to check their exact weight. At the plate he was as precise a batter as there has ever been. Williams won Triple Crowns in 1942 and '47—a season he began with the two-hit day pictured here and after which he was famously snubbed for the MVP award. In '57, at age 39 he hit .388. In '60 he belted a home run in his final at bat. Williams's career on-base percentage of .482 is the best ever. By nine points. He might have broken Babe Ruth's career home run record if he hadn't given three seasons to fighter-pilot training during World War II and then most of two other seasons to flying combat missions during the Korean War, serving as wingman to future astronaut and U.S. Senator John Glenn. Williams was the subject of legends about his eyesight that have been debunked, by him. He readily admitted he couldn't see the seams of a fastball. The true stories about Williams, though, have only grown more impressive with time.

Photograph by THE BREARLEY COLLECTION

TAKING IT TO THE STREETS

NEW YORK CITY | *June of 1947*

IN SOME RESPECTS the beauty of baseball can be seen in its physical design—for example, in the way the distances between the mound, the batter's box, and the bases produce so many game-of-inches plays at first base. But if you remove the prescribed geometry, the game, it turns out, can reveal even deeper levels of charm. In the unlikeliest of places kids armed with nothing more than a broomstick and a rubber ball have used their imaginations to construct their own private Yankee Stadiums and Ebbets Fields—with clotheslines, in the particular case of this photo, doing their best impersonation of Fourth of July bunting. By the mid-20th century New York stickball was a major pastime of city kids, as they turned apartment courtyards and lightly trafficked side streets into their own fields of dreams. Kids played the game in Boston and Chicago and Philadelphia and other urban outposts besides. And these big-city confabulations spawned cousins in the country and the suburbs, too. Whether home plate was actually a manhole cover, or a hubcap come loose, or a Frisbee dropped in the backyard grass, it became clear than even when a baseball game's layout was not a diamond, it could still be a gem.

Photograph by RALPH MORSE
THE LIFE PICTURE COLLECTION/GETTY IMAGES

1948 to 1968

Carl Yastrzemski's bat, 1967, his Triple Crown season

Golden Years

> "Our skills were as good as the men's. We just weren't strong enough to compete with them."
> —**DOTTIE KAMENSHEK**, FIRST BASEMAN AND SEVEN-TIME ALL-STAR, ALL-AMERICAN GIRLS PROFESSIONAL BASEBALL LEAGUE

A TIME TO SHINE

MIAMI | *April 11, 1948*

THE WOMEN BALLPLAYERS had to wear skirts (technically they were flared tunics with shorts), attend charm school and learn to do their makeup properly because "femininity is the keynote of our league," according to instructions the players received from the league office. "No pants-wearing, tough-talking female softballer will play on any of our four teams." But the All-American Girls Professional Baseball League survived for 12 seasons because those women delivered a product that fans could appreciate. Cubs owner Philip K. Wrigley founded the league in 1943 out of concern that manpower shortages during World War II might leave ballparks idle. Tryouts for the AAGPBL attracted 280 women to Chicago, and 60 of the best were allotted among four teams: the Rockford (Ill.) Peaches, the South Bend Blue Sox, the Racine (Wis.) Belles and the Kenosha (Wis.) Comets. (The Comets are shown here playing the Muskegon (Mich.) Lassies during spring training; the league fielded teams in 15 cities over the course of its existence.) Jimmie Foxx was the most notable of the former major leaguers who became managers. The league ran until '54, and its history was celebrated in the beloved 1992 movie *A League of Their Own*, in which some characters were based upon real players from the league. The league's players association, still active in '92 (and today), issued a statement saying that the film captured their experience, and that players argued over which of them was most like the lead characters played by Geena Davis and Lori Petty. Also, "If you asked one of the old-timers which one of them was [played by] Madonna, they will all raise their hand."

Photograph by BETTMANN/GETTY IMAGES

"I use my single windup, my double windup, my triple windup, my hesitation windup, my no windup. I also use my step-'n'-pitch-it, my submariner, my sidearmer and my bat dodger. Man's got to do what he's got to do."
—SATCHEL PAIGE

A PITCHER FOR THE AGES

MUNICIPAL STADIUM, CLEVELAND | *July of 1948*

IF HE LOOKS a bit tired, there's a reason. Satchel Paige began pitching professionally in 1926, and with his popping fastball and charismatic way he became a star attraction of the Negro leagues, occasionally telling his outfielders to sit down, so confident was he that he would strike out the next batter. When Paige wasn't playing Negro leagues games he was either barnstorming the U.S. or taking the mound in the Dominican Republic. In one exhibition he went up against a young Joe DiMaggio, who later called Paige the best pitcher he ever faced. According to Paige's own records he started 2,500 games, which sounds improbable, but then baseball's color barrier forced him to work in worlds in which strict record-keeping wasn't in the budget.

When Paige finally reached the majors in 1948, signed by Bill Veeck's Cleveland Indians, he was 42 years old. That season he went 6–1 with a 2.48 ERA. He would pitch in 179 big league games, often in relief, and was an All-Star in '52 and '53. Paige's last official major league appearance came in 1965, at age 59, when, partly as a stunt and partly to satisfy a service-time requirement for his pension eligibiity, he made a comeback on Satchel Paige Appreciation Night with the Kansas City A's. Even then his pitching, and his showmanship, were in fine form. After sitting in the bullpen in a rocking chair with a nurse beside him, he entered the game and pitched three scoreless innings against the Red Sox, allowing only one hit, to Carl Yastrzemski. Paige's career embodies what segregation took away from players, from fans and the game itself. How great would it have been to see Satchel Paige take on Babe Ruth in his prime? Paige had many sage quotes, none more poignant than: "Don't look back, something might be gaining on you."

Photograph by GEORGE SILK
THE LIFE PICTURE COLLECTION/GETTY IMAGES

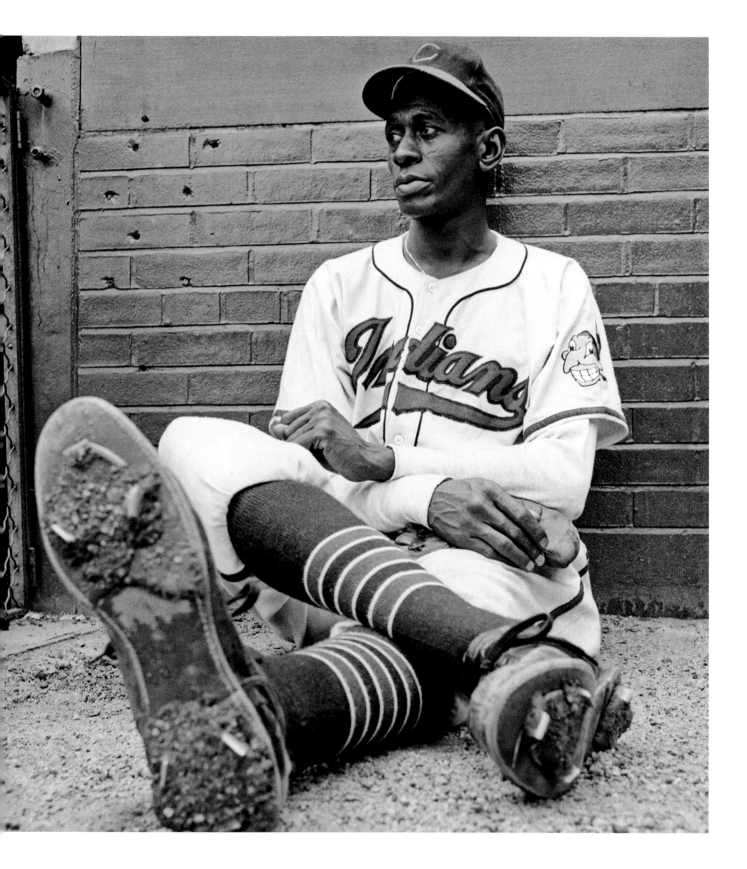

A SUNDAY LARK

SPORTSMAN'S PARK, ST. LOUIS | *August 19, 1951*

THE 1951 ST. LOUIS BROWNS were a terrible team, on their way to a 52–102 record and last place in the American League. In July, the team was sold to Bill Veeck, and the new owner decided to have a little fun and try to draw some interest to the team. Veeck treated sports as entertainment. Over the course of his decades in baseball he would send out baseball clown Max Patkin as a base coach, and in 1979 he held Disco Demolition Night, when he invited fans to bring their out-of-fashion records to the field, where they would be blown up. Veeck was a pioneer of promotion, and his most ingenious stunt involved a 43-inch batter.

Eddie Gaedel was a showman, just like Veeck. A welder by profession, he had on the side entertained in rodeos and circuses, and he was ready to play the joke all the way. Veeck waited until a weekend to sign Gaedel, which meant that baseball officials wouldn't scrutinize the contract until they came to work on Monday. That Sunday the Browns had a home doubleheader against the Tigers, and between games Gaedel was introduced to fans when he popped out of a seven-foot birthday cake. Then, in the bottom of the first inning, Gaedel, wearing the number ⅛, came to the plate. With his small strike zone (and crouched stance to boot), Gaedel walked on four pitches. He trotted to first base and was pulled for a pinch runner, accompanied by a standing ovation from the crowd. The next day American League president Will Harridge voided Gaedel's contract. Gaedel, continuing to play his part, bemoaned the unfairness of it all to the press, pointing to his 1.000 on-base percentage—a stat that remains today, unsurpassed, in the official records of Major League Baseball. Said Gaedel: "For a minute I felt like Babe Ruth."

Photograph by AP

SURVIVING THOMSON'S SHOT

POLO GROUNDS, NEW YORK CITY | *October 3, 1951*

HE LOOKED GOOD in the bullpen. Definitely better than Carl Erskine, whose curve was not popping. Both Erskine and Ralph Branca were usually starting pitchers but this was the final game in a best-of-three playoff for the National League pennant, so everyone was available. That season the Dodgers had had a 13½-game lead on Aug. 11, and the pennant didn't seem like a thing that would need saving. Then the Giants, who had not won the N.L. in 14 years, went on a 16-game winning streak, and the season ended with the two teams tied. Now here they were, and the Dodgers had a 4–2 lead with one out in the bottom of the ninth inning. The Giants had two runners on, and Branca, a three-time All-Star, was called in to relieve Don Newcombe. Bobby Thomson was at the plate for the Giants. Willie Mays was on deck. Branca got ahead 0–1 and then tried a high fastball. When Thomson hit it, leftfielder Andy Pafko ran back, thinking the ball didn't have enough to clear the wall. It did. Radio announcer Russ Hodges repeated in disbelief, *"The Giants win the pennant! The Giants win the pennant!"* He said it four times. The Giants players carried Thomson off the field. Branca *(left)* sat on the clubhouse steps.

The game was the first ever televised to a national audience, and the home run soon became known as the Miracle at Coogan's Bluff and, even more widely, as the Shot Heard 'Round the World. That night, with the wound still fresh, Branca and his fiancée, Ann (they would marry 17 days later) had dinner at a Bronx steakhouse with catcher Rube Walker and his wife. Ann's cousin, a priest, joined them. Years later Branca recalled that he asked the priest why this awful thing happened to him. The priest's answer: because Branca had the strength to handle it. "It was my salvation," Branca said. "I realized that I had done the best I could. The guy just hit a home run. He was better than I was this day. Life goes on. You don't go through it undefeated." After retirement Branca and Thomson did public appearances together. Branca gave up baseball's most famous shot, and he lived to tell about it.

Photograph by BARNEY STEIN

> "I can't very well tell my batters don't hit it to him. Wherever they hit it, he's there anyway."
> —**GIL HODGES**, MANAGER

THE CATCH

POLO GROUNDS, NEW YORK CITY | *September 29, 1954*

WILLIE MAYS BUILT his legend in the outfield. The way he hit was the stuff of greatness—660 home runs, 3,283 hits—but it was in the grassy expanse of the Polo Grounds that he performed his magic. As a rookie in 1951 in a game against Pittsburgh, Mays ran down a ball and, seeing it was arcing away from his glove, reached up and made the catch with his bare hand. Against the Dodgers that summer he snared a long drive by Carl Furillo while speeding away from the infield, then turned and threw a whistling fly that got the runner at home. Mays made plays others could not, and he did it with a palpable energy—*Say Hey!*—with a love of the game. This was a man who, even on a morning when he had a doubleheader at the Polo Grounds awaiting him, would hear the neighborhood kids knocking at his window in Harlem and go out to join them for stickball on the street.

Mays made his most famous catch—this one—in the 1954 World Series. It was the eighth inning of Game 1, the score was tied, and Mays was cheating up in centerfield so he might be in position to make a throw home. The Giants hadn't won a World Series in 21 years, and they were not expected to win this one. When Vic Wertz of the favored Indians drove a ball deep to center, Mays turned, galloping with his back to home plate and, in a feat that only becomes more improbable the more you study it, caught the ball without turning his head. Cap falling off, he whirled and threw the ball in, saving a run. The Giants won the game. They won the Series. And an immortal baseball moment was secure.

Photograph by NEW YORK DAILY NEWS ARCHIVE/GETTY IMAGES

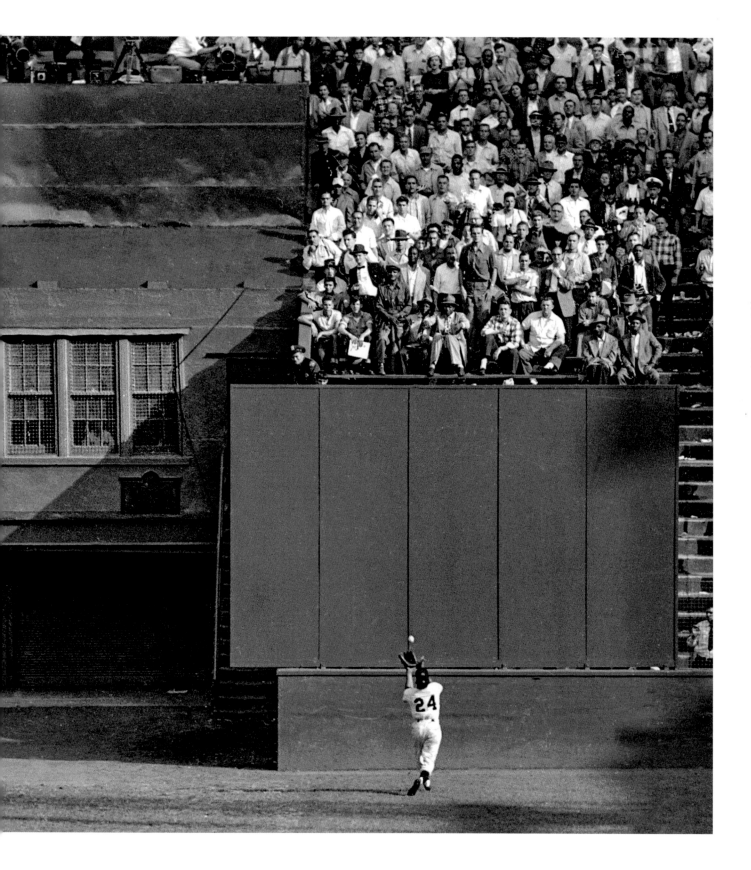

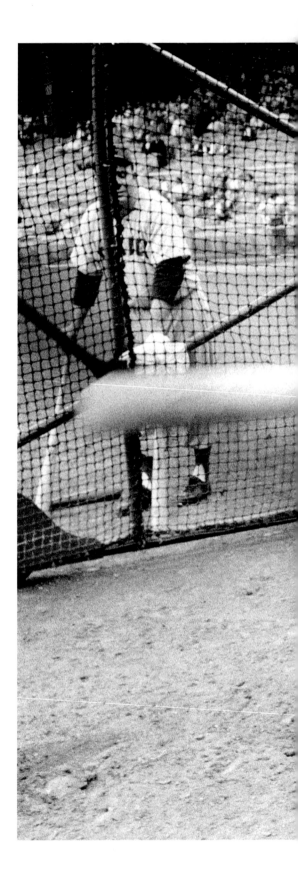

MR. CUB,
MR. SUNSHINE

POLO GROUNDS, NEW YORK CITY | *June 4, 1955*

ERNIE BANKS DIDN'T didn't particularly love baseball as a kid, at least not at first. When his father bought him a glove and ball at age eight, he would only consent to play if his dad bribed him with spare change. But as an adult, Banks treated each day at the ballpark as a treasure. He could often be heard asking, "What can be better than being outdoors and playing this wonderful game?" His famous optimism withstood—and came to seem like a response to—playing on Chicago Cubs teams that did an awful lot of losing. Banks began his career in the Negro leagues with the Kansas City Monarchs, but after returning from two years in the Army, his rights were sold to Chicago in September 1953, and that month he became the Cubs' first black player. He won MVP awards in '58 and '59 on teams that finished in fifth place in the National League. It wasn't until '63 that Banks played on a team with a winning record. And although he hit for power better than any shortstop before him ever had, and wound up with 512 career home runs, Banks never in his 19-year career participated in a playoff game. "Sometimes I'm at a Hall of Fame reunion," Banks said later in life, "and I'll look around and see I'm the only one in the room who never played in a World Series. I've had nightmares about it." But on the field those misgivings did not show. Mr. Cub arrived at the ballpark every day, sometimes sounding his famous line: "It's a beautiful day for a ball game. Let's play two."

Photograph by YALE JOEL

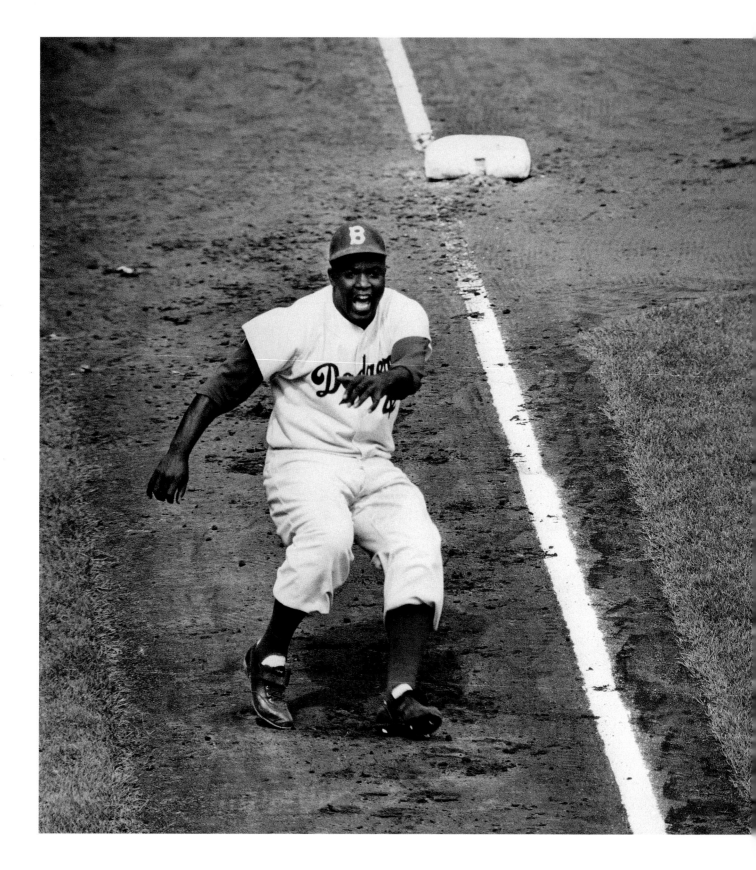

THE PATH OF A PIONEER

EBBETS FIELD, BROOKLYN, N.Y. | *September 30, 1955*

BASEBALL'S PROHIBITION against fielding African-American players was never written as official policy, but the so-called "gentleman's agreement" was strictly enforced until 1945, when Dodgers general manager Branch Rickey decided that he was going to sign baseball's first African-American player. He identified Jackie Robinson as an ideal candidate. Robinson was known to sports fans from his days as a four-sport letterman at UCLA, and he had already proved that he could perform in the spotlight. He was an exciting player with excellent speed. Furthermore, Robinson didn't drink or smoke, and he was about to become a married man. In a face-to-face meeting Rickey tested Robinson with racial slurs, wanting to see that Robinson had the temperament not to fight back. Robinson spent the '46 season with the Montreal Royals, a Brooklyn farm team, and then made his major league debut on April 15, 1947, at age 28, facing a pressure no athlete had ever known, representing not only himself and his team but also his race. After an up-and-down start Robinson went on a 14-game hitting streak in May and hurtled on to the '47 Rookie of the Year award, showing that African-Americans could compete, and draw at the ticket window. The former track star electrified the game with his baserunning. In his 10-year Hall of Fame career Robinson led the league in steals twice and stole home a National League record 19 times, including during the 1955 World Series (pictured here) which he helped the Dodgers to win. By 1959 every major league team had an African-American player on its roster. Baseball's unwritten rule had been erased.

Photograph by RALPH MORSE
THE LIFE PICTURE COLLECTION/GETTY IMAGES

PRESIDENTIAL STRIKES

GRIFFITH STADIUM, WASHINGTON, D.C. | *April 17, 1956*

THE INTERSECTION BETWEEN baseball and politics is usually brief and ceremonial, though not always. Presidents have been throwing out pitches on Opening Day since William Howard Taft did it in 1910 (Dwight Eisenhower is in action at left), and have been hosting baseball's champs since Calvin Coolidge welcomed the 1924 Senators. During Ronald Reagan's presidency in the 1980s it became de rigueur for World Series winners to visit the White House for banter, congratulations and photo ops. But on occasion the baseball-and-commander-in-chief linkages have had more gravity. In January 1942, after the Japanese attack on Pearl Harbor, commissioner Kenesaw Mountain Landis wrote to President Franklin Delano Roosevelt, asking whether baseball should continue as the nation prepared for war. "I honestly feel that it would be best for the country to keep baseball going," Roosevelt wrote. "[People] ought to have a chance for recreation and for taking their minds off their work." Another crisis provided the backdrop for a presidential pitch that felt significant. Forty-nine days after the terror attacks of Sept. 11, 2001, George W. Bush came to Yankee Stadium for Game 3 of the '01 World Series, After warming up beneath the stands and being warned by Yankees captain Derek Jeter that fans would boo if he threw badly, Bush walked to the mound wearing a jacket from the New York Fire Department. A former minority owner of the Texas Rangers, Bush delivered a 60-foot, six-inch strike. He was a Republican in a city that tended to vote Democratic, but that night all Bush heard from New Yorkers were chants of "U.S.A., U.S.A."

Photograph by MARK KAUFFMAN

PERFECT

YANKEE STADIUM, BRONX, N.Y. | *October 8, 1956*

IN 1954, HIS SECOND season in the majors, Don Larsen, pitching for the Baltimore Orioles, went 3–21 with a 4.37 ERA. That is far from perfect. The Yankees nonetheless acquired the 6' 4" righthander before the '55 season and he would reward their faith, putting up winning records in four of his five years in New York. Still, Larsen (nickname: Gooney Bird, career record 81–91), was an unlikely candidate to throw the only perfect game—and no-hitter—in World Series history.

In Game 2 of the 1956 series against the Brooklyn Dodgers, Larsen had lasted less than two innings. He figured that if he was handed the ball again, it would be as a reliever. But Yankees manager Casey Stengel surprised Larsen on the day of Game 5 at Yankee Stadium leaving a ball in Larsen's shoe to indicate he would start—against a Dodgers lineup flush with boldface names: Jackie Robinson, Duke Snider, Roy Campanella, Carl Furillo, Pee Wee Reese. Larsen said he had the best stuff of his career that day. He also had help. Two Dodgers hit balls of home run distance that went foul by inches. A deep shot by Gil Hodges in the fifth inning was caught by Mickey Mantle in full stride with his back to the plate. In the dugout after the seventh with the Yankees leading 2–0, Larsen said to Mantle, "Look at that. Two more innings. Wouldn't it be something?" The Dodgers ninth began with a fly ball from Furillo, then a groundout by Campanella. Pinch hitter Dale Mitchell, the last batter, went down looking.

Larsen's achievement is singular, but give some credit to the man embracing him in this photo: Yogi Berra, who caught a career 184 shutouts (seven by Larsen) and won a record 10 World Series and a record 14 league championships. Berra guided many to their best.

Photograph by BETTMANN/GETTY IMAGES

"They had a tunnel back to the clubhouse,
and I took off and got into the champagne.
I didn't even see him cross home plate."
—**JOE GIBBON**, PIRATES PITCHER

MAZ'S MAGIC MOMENT

FORBES FIELD, PITTSBURGH | *October 13, 1960*

THE CUMULATIVE SCORE of the seven games of the 1960 World Series was: Yankees 55, Pirates 27. That imbalance, thanks to three blowout wins by New York, underscores why the Yankees were the Goliath in that matchup. There was also the history. The Pirates had not won a World Series since '25, while the Yankees had taken seven of the previous 11. But Pittsburgh made it to the deciding game and even led 9–7 in the top half of the ninth inning, before the Yankees, as was their wont, rallied to tie the score.

That turn of events got Pirates second baseman Bill Mazeroski thinking about Yankees dominance. As a kid in Ohio, he had seen them beat up on his beloved Cleveland Indians time and time again. Here, as he led off the bottom of the ninth against righthander Ralph

Terry, was the chance to exact some revenge. He did it, connecting on the second pitch, a low fastball. Yogi Berra, playing in leftfield, thought he had a shot at playing a carom off the 18-foot-high wall but instead saw the ball graze the ivy as it sailed over for a game-ending home run. It remains the only walk-off home run in the history of World Series Game 7s, and it would help propel Mazeroski, known mainly for his defense, to the Hall of Fame. As Mazeroski rounded third, fans raced onto the field, and Pittsburgh began to celebrate. Office workers, emptying filing cabinets, threw so much paper onto the streets that the trolleys couldn't run. The joy was overwhelming. The Pirates had beaten the Yankees.

Photograph by HARRY HARRIS/AP/SHUTTERSTOCK

THE ROAD TO 61

MEMORIAL STADIUM, BALTIMORE | *September 20, 1961*

ROGER MARIS WASN'T born for the spotlight, but he landed in it in 1961, suddenly facing hordes of reporters in every city as he threatened to break the single-season home run record held by Babe Ruth. Yankees teammate Mickey Mantle also had a shot at the mark, and their race against each other and the game's most beloved figure became the story of the summer. Mantle knew how to handle the media with an easy grin. Maris didn't. In Chicago a reporter asked Maris if he really wanted to break Ruth's record. "Damn right," Maris said. "What I mean is," the reporter said, offering a clearer prompt, "Ruth was a great man." Maris snapped back, "Maybe I'm not a great man, but I damn well want to break the record." Maris's brusque manner set him up as the saga's villain. Comments like these from Hall of Famer Rogers Hornsby didn't help: "It would be a shame if Ruth's record got broken by a .270 hitter."

Maris, who never hit as many as 40 homers in any other season, sometimes hid in the training room to avoid the media. He slept poorly and lost clumps of hair. That season was the first year in which baseball had extended its schedule from 154 to 162 games, and commissioner Ford Frick declared in mid-season that for Maris to be the one-and-only record-holder, he needed to break Ruth's mark in 154 games. Maris hit his 59th in game 154 and is pictured here in the locker room afterward. (Mantle, en route to 54 home runs, was hampered by injury and was in and out of the lineup toward the end of the season.) Number 61 for Maris came in the final game of the year. He entered the books qualified as the 162-game record-holder, his name listed below Ruth's.

Photograph by HERB SCHARFMAN

> "Casey knew his baseball. He only made it look like he was fooling around. He knew every move that was ever invented."
> —**SPARKY ANDERSON**, REDS AND TIGERS MANAGER

A MIGHTY CASEY

POLO GROUNDS, NEW YORK CITY | *June 9, 1963*

HE HAD JOE DIMAGGIO. He had Mickey Mantle. He had Yogi Berra. And then, at the end, he had "Marvelous" Marv Throneberry. Casey Stengel's baseball life, which began in 1912 when he played outfield for the Brooklyn Dodgers, ascended to its greatest heights from '49 to '60, when he managed Yankees teams that were stocked with Hall of Famers and won seven World Series. The Pirates' Bill Mazeroski's home run in the '60 World Series ended Stengel's tenure, and he spent a year working at a California bank owned by his wife's family. In '62 he was lured back to baseball to manage the expansion Mets. Stengel was adored in New York not just for his winning history but for his comic persona. He would drop lines such as, "The secret of managing is to keep the guys who hate you away from the guys who are undecided." He

observed that, "You have to have a catcher, otherwise you will have a lot of passed balls." So Stengel spent the final years of his career as the public face of a team that was hilariously inept, defined by such acts as Throneberry's legging out a triple without touching either first or second base. In that first season his Mets lost 120 games, the most in baseball history, and Jimmy Breslin's chronicle of that season was titled *Can't Anybody Here Play This Game?*, a line he attributed to Stengel. The Old Perfessor helmed the Mets for 3½ losing seasons, until he fell and broke his hip. Still, the franchise gave him a ring when the team won the World Series in '69, and he is one of only four Mets to have his number retired. You could look it up.

Photograph by NEIL LEIFER

THE MAN

BUSCH STADIUM, ST. LOUIS | *September 29, 1963*

ONE OF THE EARLIEST of Stan Musial's many fans was Joe Barboa, a neighbor in Donora, the Western Pennsylvania mill town where Musial grew up. Barboa, a semi-pro player, would come home exhausted from a shift at the zinc mill and find seven-year-old Stan waiting to play ball. Barboa would accommodate him, he told SI in 1957, because "I never saw anything like him. Everything he did was right—the way he'd throw, the way he'd bat, the way he'd run. I used to play with him just to watch him." Doing everything right became the way for Musial, who never knew a down season. From '41 to '58, he hit at least .310 every year, During a peak stretch, from '43 to '52, he led the majors six times in both batting average and OPS. A three-time National League MVP, Musial stood up there in a unique, hunch-backed, bat-high stance and finished his career with 1,815 hits on the road and 1,815 hits at home—the last being a grounder in '63 that got by Reds rookie second baseman Pete Rose, who would become the only National Leaguer ever with more career hits than Musial. This photo was taken before that final game. "Here stands baseball's perfect knight," baseball commissioner Ford Frick said about Musial in an inscription that adorns the statue of Musial near the ballpark in St Louis. Musial was married to his wife Lillian for 71 years, and he had a similarly long and harmonious union with the Cardinals organization after his playing career ended. He was an unstinting spreader of joy, and his talents included playing the harmonica. On a few occasions he opened the Hall of Fame induction ceremonies with a rendition of *Take Me Out to the Ball Game*, the kind of thing that gets everyone in the mood.

Photograph by RICH CLARKSON

PURE GREATNESS

DODGER STADIUM, LOS ANGELES | *October 6, 1963*

SANDY KOUFAX HAD been merely good through the first seven seasons of his career, but beginning in 1962 he went on one of the greatest runs any pitcher has known. Suddenly, having tweaked the delivery on his fastball, the Dodgers lefty was all but unhittable. From '62 to '66 he won three Cy Young awards and led the league in ERA each year. He went 111–34 in that time, pitching four no-hitters (one a perfect game) before retiring at age 30 because of arthritis in his pitching elbow. In the '63 World Series against the Yankees, Koufax's mastery was on full display. He won two starts against Whitey Ford, including a 2–1 win in Game 4 that completed the Series sweep *(right)*. In the '65 Series Koufax again won two games (both shutouts) and took a loss in Game 2, when he allowed a single run. But his most remembered World Series performance may be the game in the '65 Series that he *didn't* pitch. Koufax informed the Dodgers that he would not be available for Game 1 because it fell on Yom Kippur, the holiest day of the Jewish calendar, which is marked by fasting, atonement and rest. At the time little fuss was made over Koufax's choice. He had missed regular-season games for religious reasons before and the Dodgers had Don Drysdale, a nine-time All-Star, to start Game 1. (Drysdale was shelled, after which he reportedly joked to manager Walter Alston, "I bet you wish I were Jewish too.") But Koufax's stand became a celebrated moment. He showed that you could be a ballplayer and an American and a Jew, and do it all the right way.

Photograph by NEIL LEIFER

STORYTELLER

DODGER STADIUM, LOS ANGELES | *April 16, 1964*

VIN SCULLY WAS calling a Dodgers home game in 1960 when, leafing through some game notes, he realized that it was the birthday of umpire Frank Secory, and he decided to have a little fun. He told his fans, many of whom were listening at the stadium on transistor radios, "As soon as the inning is over, I'll count to three, and on three everybody yell, 'Happy birthday, Frank!'" When the birthday shouts came out from the stands, Secory looked up, shocked. The moment demonstrated the connection that Scully, and baseball's greatest voices, have with their audiences. The game, with its ample pauses, is built for radio, and announcers can become as identified with their teams as any player. It has been true of Ernie Harwell in Detroit, Marty Brennaman in Cincinnati, Jack Buck in St. Louis and Harry Kalas in Philadelphia.

Scully began with the Dodgers in 1950, when he was 22 and the team was in Brooklyn. He came along to Los Angeles and manned the microphone for 67 seasons, until he retired in 2016. From early radio to the Internet streams of MLB.com, he told fans, "It's time for Dodger baseball!" and narrated the exploits of Jackie Robinson, Steve Garvey and Yasiel Puig, of Sandy Koufax and Clayton Kershaw. He called Don Larsen's perfect game, Hank Aaron's 715th home run and Kirk Gibson's 1988 World Series homer. He knew when to illuminate big moments and when to leave them alone. And he could make small moments shine too. He once told his audiences that Andre Dawson, because of a bruised knee, was listed as day-to-day, and then added, "Aren't we all?"

Photograph by PHIL BATH

"Fidel Castro never had an appointment before 3 p.m. . . . and what he'd do for several hours before he saw anybody was read the newspapers. So he knew all the standings, the batting averages. He was a prolific follower of U.S. baseball."

—**BILL RICHARDSON**, GOVERNOR OF NEW MEXICO

POLITICAL HARDBALL

CUBA | *June 15, 1964*

THE TRUTH ABOUT the baseball prowess of Fidel Castro is slippery. The oft-told myth is that he had a live arm, major-league potential and was scouted by the Yankees. The course of history could have changed if he had chosen baseball over politics. The reality is more pedestrian: Castro played baseball as a schoolboy, and perhaps participated in intramural games while a law school student. Also, in 1959, as part of an effort to support baseball and lift national pride soon after becoming prime minister of Cuba, the 6' 2" righthander pitched a successful exhibition inning or two for a pickup club, Los Barbudos (the Bearded Ones), in front of a crowd of 25,000 in Havana.

Certainly Castro, who ruled Cuba from 1959 to 2011, loved baseball. In a 2008 story in SPORTS ILLUSTRATED, former Cardinals pitcher Rene Arocha said he heard reports of Castro's showing up at a baseball stadium at two or three in the morning to take batting practice: "The story is that Fidel would be at the plate yelling, 'Throw it fast!' while an escort would stand next to the mound whispering, 'Throw it slow.' "

Castro's lasting influence on baseball is the players that he kept on his island while relations with the U.S. remained chilled. Many of the Latino players who reached the majors pre-Castro came from Cuba, and there were some who defected during his reign. But only recently has the flow resumed: Aroldis Chapman, Yoenis Cespedes, José Fernandez, Yasiel Puig. For decades Cuba's big bats and arms remained stuck on an island, 90 miles from America.

Photograph by JUNG/ULLSTEIN BILD/GETTY IMAGES

"Bob Gibson is the luckiest pitcher in baseball. He is always pitching when the other team doesn't score any runs."
—**TIM MCCARVER**, CARDINALS CATCHER

GAME-CHANGER

BUSCH STADIUM, ST. LOUIS | *October 8, 1964*

WHEN JOE TORRE caught Bob Gibson at the 1965 All-Star Game, the pitcher wouldn't speak to him. Not on the mound, not in the shower afterward. They didn't have any beef; the problem was that Torre played on another team (the Braves), and Gibson, a Cardinal his whole career, didn't consort with the enemy. The enemy was anyone who might attempt to hit his pitching—especially if he had the gall to crowd the plate or, if he was really asking for it, hit a home run. Then Gibson would get quite angry with him. "The part of pitching that separates the stars from everyone else is about 90% mental," Gibson said. "I considered it so important to mess with a batter's head without letting him inside mine." His toughness wasn't an act. In July 1967, Roberto Clemente hit a line drive that broke Gibson's shin. Gibson threw three more pitches, only leaving the game after the bone had fully snapped.

Gibson came back to win three World Series games that year, all complete games—and part of a streak of seven World Series wins. But he was never better than in 1968, when he set a post–Dead Ball era record with a 1.12 ERA. He completed 28 of his 34 starts that year and was pinch-hit for in the other six, which means that for an entire season he was never asked to leave the mound. Due to the dominance of Gibson and others in "The Year of the Pitcher," the mound was lowered from 15 to 10 inches the following season, meaning that his ERA feat, which hasn't been threatened, may never be surpassed.

Photograph by MARVIN E. NEWMAN

"The Eiffel Tower is nice, but you can't play ball there."
—ROY HOFHEINZ, CREATOR OF THE ASTRODOME, BRAGGING ABOUT THE STRUCTURE TO HERVÉ ALPHAND, FRANCE'S AMBASSADOR TO THE U.S.

INSIDE BASEBALL

ASTRODOME, HOUSTON | *April 12, 1965*

FOR A TIME after the Astrodome opened in 1965, the parking attendants wore spaceman suits. Houston is home to NASA's Johnson Space Center, and the suits also matched the sci-fi feel of this stadium of the future. Billed as the Eighth Wonder of the World, the Astrodome was sports' first enclosed and air-conditioned stadium. The dome, which cost $37 million (about $292 million in 2018 dollars), was built as a defense against Houston's sweltering summers. The first regular-season game *(shown at right)* was against the Phillies, and the playing surface was a Bermuda grass, engineered to thrive indoors with the aid of the sun that would shine through the roof's 4,596 lucite skylights. But outfielders complained that they were losing the ball in the glare. So the skylights were painted over. The grass died. In 1966 the field was resurfaced with ChemGrass—soon given the more welcoming name, AstroTurf. Other cities followed, building domes of their own, for baseball or for football. Even newly built open-air stadiums carpeted their fields with artificial turf. The false grass was hard and the ball could bounce unnaturally high and skip unnaturally fast.

Then in 1992 the Orioles moved into Camden Yards, with its natural grass and quaint irregular features, and soon the dome and turf trend was out and the retro look was in. The Astros left the dome after the '99 season and now the majors' only fully enclosed stadium is Tampa Bay's Tropicana Field. The Astros' new park has a retractable roof—one of six in baseball. Those roofs are closed as infrequently as possible.

Photograph by ROBERT RIGER/GETTY IMAGES

MICKEY, LATE IN THE GAME

YANKEE STADIUM, BRONX, N.Y. | *June 20, 1965*

MANY PHOTOS OF Mickey Mantle present him as the quintessential Beautiful Youth. From Oklahoma, he was boyish, handsome and strapping, and he hit jaw-dropping home runs that inspired the invention of the tape-measure shot. And Mantle was no one-trick pony. He was quick. He switch-hit. In 1956 he won the Triple Crown with 52 HRs, 130 RBIs and a .353 average. He played in 12 World Series in his first 14 seasons, winning seven. He was golden.

This photo is different. This is Mickey Mantle in 1965, when that gold was beginning to wear. He was 33, and that year he hit .255, which was then a career worst, by a lot. He had only 19 home runs in 122 games, and the Yankees went 77–85. In this picture Mickey Mantle is throwing his helmet in disgust—he has just grounded out—showing the frustration known to any athlete who reaches an age when his body won't do what it used to. It must have been particularly painful for Mantle, who once did whatever he wanted.

It also hurt because for Mantle his struggles were, to a degree, self-inflicted. In 1994 he wrote in a confessional piece in SPORTS ILLUSTRATED, "God gave me a great body to play with, and I didn't take care of it. And I blame a lot of it on alcohol. Everybody tries to make the excuse that injuries shortened my career. Truth is, after I'd had a knee operation, the doctors would give me rehab work to do, but I wouldn't do it. I'd be out drinking." So, even with 536 home runs and a plaque in the Hall of Fame, it may have been more than a helmet that Mantle threw away.

Photograph by JOHN DOMINIS
THE LIFE PICTURE COLLECTION/GETTY IMAGES

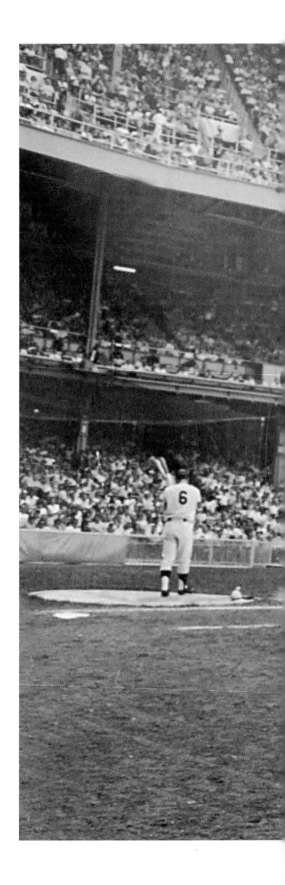

AN AWFUL OUTBURST

CANDLESTICK PARK, SAN FRANCISCO | *August 22, 1965*

BASEBALL CAN BE the most pastoral of team sports, but it
sometimes shows its capacity for violence, and rarely more so
than in a 1965 game between the Los Angeles Dodgers and the
San Francisco Giants. A Friday night game earlier in the series
had become testy when batters for both teams were accused of
intentionally hitting catchers on the backswing. On Sunday the
nastiness resumed when Giants starter Juan Marichal brushed back
a batter in each of the second and third innings. When Marichal
came to bat in the bottom of the third, Dodgers catcher John
Roseboro wanted pitcher Sandy Koufax to retaliate, but that wasn't
Koufax's style. So Roseboro asked Koufax to throw a curveball high
and inside. The catcher then buzzed Marichal on the toss back to
the mound. You know who didn't like that plan? Marichal. After
Roseboro's throw grazed his earlobe, Marichal turned on Roseboro,
words were exchanged, and Marichal raised the bat and brought it
down on Roseboro's head, twice. The benches cleared, and players
fought for 14 minutes. Blood ran down Roseboro's face and chest
protector. It was a horrifying moment, but with a strangely sweet
coda. In the early '80s the men made peace. Roseboro, who had
needed 14 stitches and missed two games after the bludgeoning, felt
the incident was keeping Marichal out of the Baseball Hall of Fame
and decided to publicly campaign on Marichal's behalf. Marichal
then did get in, and when Roseboro died in 2002, Marichal spoke
at his funeral. He declared that Roseboro's forgiving him was one
of the best things that had happened in his life. After that burst of
anger, its perpetrators found peace.

Photograph by NEIL LEIFER

COMING TO TOWN

PEACHTREE STREET, ATLANTA | *April 12, 1966*

THERE WAS A judge in Milwaukee who tried to rain on the aftermath of this parade. This was the day of the Braves' first game in their new home, Atlanta, and the city welcomed the franchise with a caravan down Peachtree Street to Atlanta Stadium. The next day in Wisconsin, circuit judge Elmer W. Roller decreed that if baseball didn't grant Milwaukee an expansion franchise by May 18—that is, about a month after this happy procession—the Braves, who had played in Milwaukee would have to come back home. The Braves had been in Wisconsin since 1953 after moving from Boston, and this was an era in which the baseball map was changing rapidly. The Giants and Dodgers had opened up the California market in '58, with the expansion Angels joining them three years later. The Philadelphia A's had moved to Kansas City in '55, and in '61 the Washington Senators became the Minnesota Twins. Houston and New York had received expansion franchises in 1962. Four more cities would receive them in '69.

The Braves, under new ownership and facing falling attendance, moved to Atlanta to take advantage of a growing market and to become baseball's first team in the Southeast. The appeal of Judge Roller's ruling advanced quickly to the Wisconsin Supreme Court, which narrowly affirmed baseball's right to place franchises wherever it pleased. Milwaukee did, of course, get baseball back again, in 1970, when the Seattle Pilots, bankrupt after one season, became the Brewers. Milwaukee was big league once again while over in Atlanta the Braves, fresh off a playoff appearance, were feeling right at home.

Photograph by NEIL LEIFER

SPRING AWAKENINGS

AL LOPEZ FIELD, TAMPA | *March of 1967*

GETTING BACK TO fundamentals is the major occupation of spring training, and not just for players. For fans who make it through the barren winter by counting down the days to when pitchers and catchers report, it's the chance to visit a small ballpark in a warm location and see veterans and rookies practice fielding grounders, just like Little Leaguers do. Spring training is a revitalizing ritual, as valuable to the baseball psyche as it is to the players' physiques. Back in the days when salaries were lower and players spent their offseasons working in taverns and auto repair shops, they needed spring training to snap their bodies back into shape and refresh their hand-eye coordination. The ritual of heading south for these camps began in 1886 when the Chicago White Stockings went to Hot Springs, Ark., and the Philadelphia Quakers went to Charleston, S.C. Early on, teams were spread around the South. The Cincinnati Reds, for instance, held their camps at locations such as Mobile, Shreveport, La., and Waxahachie, Texas, before settling, as most teams did, in the Sunshine State. These Florida teams played an exhibition schedule catering to a population rich with retirees and vacationers and the competition became known as the Grapefruit League. The Reds, pictured here, were in Florida (at locations including Tampa, Plant City and Sarasota) every year from 1923 until 2008, when the team, like many others, pulled up stakes for Arizona's burgeoning Cactus League. Arizona had sunshine and retirees too, as well as new ballparks to accommodate all those wanting a little taste of rejuvenation.

Photograph by NEIL LEIFER

CROWD PLEASER

FENWAY PARK, BOSTON | *October 1, 1967*

A RED SOX home game was once an easy ticket. In 1966 the Sox were near the bottom of the league in attendance, averaging only 10,014 fans a game. The team was terrible that year, finishing in ninth place in its eighth straight losing season, and prospects didn't seem much better for '67. But that year Boston began to turn it all around. The offense was sparked by Triple Crown winner Carl Yastrzemski, and the pitching was led by Cy Young winner Jim Lonborg. Excitement peaked on the last day of the season, with the Red Sox needing a win for a chance at the World Series, and Lonborg on the mound against the Minnesota Twins— the team locked with Boston at the top of the standings. Lonborg keyed an offensive rally with a bunt single in the sixth inning, and finished a complete-game win when a bloop landed in the glove of shortstop Rico Petrocelli. The Red Sox still needed a loss by Detroit, later that day to clinch the pennant outright, but a tie was secure, and the celebration would not wait. "It's pandemonium on the field!" said Boston broadcaster Ned Martin, as frenzied fans swarmed Lonborg, pulling buttons from his uniform, the festivities flirting with the feral. The Red Sox had not won a pennant in 21 years and Bostonians were referring to the season as The Impossible Dream.

The Tigers did lose later that day, and the Sox met St. Louis in the World Series. The Cardinals found motivation when Red Sox manager Dick Williams, asked about his Game 7 lineup, replied, "Lonborg and champagne." But Lonborg, who had won his two other World Series starts, lost Game 7, pitching on just two days rest. The Cardinals popped corks while Boston tasted disappointment, but still, the chase was on, for a city and for its fans. Those Fenway seats would become very hard to get: The Red Sox hold the record across all sports for most consecutive sellouts, 820, from 2003 to 2013.

Photograph by WALTER IOOSS JR.

1969
to
1993

Rickey Henderson's shoe, 1991, worn for his record-breaking 939th stolen base

Expanding Influence

THE LABOR REVOLUTION

U.S. DISTRICT COURT, NEW YORK CITY | *May 21, 1970*

MARVIN MILLER HAD a simple explanation for why he was able to effect so much change for baseball players: Baseball's labor rules were terrible, he felt, and there was much room for improvement. Miller was hired by the players in 1966, coming from the United Steelworkers union. At the time the players' minimum salary was $6,000, and had gone up only $1,000 since '47. Player grievances were heard by the commissioner, who is an employee of the owners, rather than by an independent arbitrator. The greatest limit on players was the reserve clause, which tied a player to a single team until he was traded or released. This rendered players powerless in salary negotiations.

Miller changed all of that. This photo shows Miller *(with the mustache)* and outfielder Curt Flood *(behind him)*. Flood, whom the previous year had been traded against his wishes from the Cardinals to the Phillies, was the first player to challenge baseball's reserve clause. His bid, which went to the U.S. Supreme Court, was unsuccessful, but a few years later, thanks to an arbitrator's ruling in a case involving pitchers Andy Messersmith and Dave McNally, the reserve clause was deemed invalid. Beginning in '76, players, within certain service-time guidelines, could become free agents and sell their services for as much as the market would bear. The game would never be the same. It was under Miller that baseball endured its first player strikes, in '72 and, most notably, a 50-day stoppage in the middle of the '81 season. He retired as head of the baseball union in '83, having fundamentally altered baseball and having set an example of collective bargaining that athletes in all sports would follow.

Photograph by BETTMANN/GETTY IMAGES

134

GAME SIX

FENWAY PARK, BOSTON | *October 21, 1975*

OF COURSE THE GESTURES of a man hopping (and wiggling and waving) down the first base line have nothing to do with the flight path of a ball careening toward leftfield. But in a way the power of Carlton Fisk's gesticulations as he attempted to will his home run fair (it worked!) in Game 6 of the 1975 World Series are still being felt. That night, in Fisk's hometown on Charlestown, N.H.—a town stocked with Red Sox fans—a man went running to the church steeple at 1:07 a.m. to ring the bells and let the town know that a local boy had made good. Fisk's 12th-inning shot (struck off righty reliever Pat Darcy) ended one of most remarkable games in baseball history, forced a Game 7 with the powerful Reds, and put the Red Sox on the verge of winning a title for the first time in 57 years. Though Boston would lose that deciding game, and Cincinnati would deliver the first of its consecutive championships, that home run remains the Series's lasting image and it capped a drama that fundamentally changed baseball on television.

Some of the influence was on presentation—the Boston catcher demonstrated the power of the reaction shot. But even bigger was the effect on scheduling. Game 6 had been set for a Saturday afternoon, before days of rain pushed it to Tuesday night. This wasn't the first World Series game played at night, but it was the first Game 6, and fans saw a back-and-forth thriller. In the eighth Boston's Bernie Carbo hit a game-tying three-run homer. Dwight Evans made a huge catch in the 11th. Then came Fisk. The drama was eaten up by 76 million viewers (35% of the U.S. population), which ensured that so many other future World Series heroics would also take place past the stroke of midnight.

Photograph by HARRY CABLUCK/AP/SHUTTERSTOCK

"There's nothing contrived about Fidrych, and that's what makes him a beautiful person. There's an electricity that he brings out in everyone, the players and the fans."
—**RUSTY STAUB**, TIGERS OUTFIELDER

RARE BIRD

PHOTO STUDIO, NEW YORK CITY | *January 30, 1977*

MARK FIDRYCH WAS NOT like the other players. One look at him on the mound told you that. He felt everything. The energy of the crowd seemed to vibrate through his long limbs as he stretched and gyrated before a pitch. If he saw a cleat mark by the rubber, he would drop to the knees to smooth the dirt before he threw. His most noted idiosyncrasy was that he would talk to the baseball—and though he later said he was really talking to himself, the ball seemed to be intimately involved in these conversations. In 1976 Fidrych, nicknamed the Bird for his resemblance to the *Sesame Street* character, was an unexpected pleasure, both for baseball fans and for a Tigers team that hadn't expected the 6'3" righty to even make the roster. But make it he did, and then the phenomenon began. Fidrych's first start was a complete game. Later, in a widely watched, nationally telecast night game against the Yankees, he threw another complete game win and the home fans called him out for one curtain call after another, a stadium full of fans not wanting to let him go. He was the All-Star Game's starting pitcher, and he led the majors in ERA at 2.34 while going 19–9. Opponents worried that Fidrych, with his shenanigans, was trying to hypnotize them.

He was such a cultural phenomenon that he made the cover of *Rolling Stone* as well as SI. But it was not to last. After pitching 250⅓ innings as a rookie, Fidrych pitched less than that over his remaining four seasons combined. First it was a knee injury, then the shoulder, and then he was done, the brevity of his career only confirming the delicate and unusual nature of this particular bird.

Photograph by LANE STEWART

THE STORY OF OH

KORAKUEN STADIUM, TOKYO | *June 4, 1977*

HE STOOD AT the plate as if in a yoga pose, lifting his front leg at the knee as the pitcher went into his motion. The leg came down when Sadaharu Oh unleashed a swing that was one of the mightiest in baseball. Oh developed the one-legged flamingo stance with hitting coach Hiroshi Arakawa, a man of broad interests who drew on ideas from martial arts and kabuki theater in the quest to help Oh, who three seasons into his career, was a mediocre and frustrated player in Japan's Nippon Professional Baseball league. The two tried many stances before arriving at this one, with the lift. It worked. Using this new approach, Oh won five batting titles and two triple crowns—and hit more home runs than anyone else in the history of professional baseball. *Oh* means king in Japanese.

He played his entire career for the Yomiuri Giants, and from 1959 to '80, when he retired at age 40, Oh hit 868 home runs. That's more than MLB record holder Barry Bonds (762) and much more than the 657 hit by Katsuya Nomura, number 2 on Japan's career list. In a book Oh co-wrote after retiring, *A Zen Way of Baseball*, he described the act of hitting this way: "In the midst of chanting and cheering crowds, colors, noises, hot and cold weather, the glare of lights, or rain on my skin, there was only this noiseless, colorless, heatless void in which the pitcher and I together enacted our certain preordained ritual of the home run."

Is Oh the true home run king? In a 2007 *Los Angeles Times* interview, he said with typical modesty: "The Japanese media want to describe me as the true record holder. But I never considered myself that way." In 1989 Oh and Hank Aaron partnered to found the World Children's Baseball Fair, an annual event that promotes the sport around the world. Whatever Oh's crown, he wears it lightly.

Photograph by TAKEO TANUMA

KICKING BUTTS

MCKECHNIE FIELD, BRADENTON, FLORIDA | *March of 1980*

DAVE PARKER WAS the first baseball player to be paid a million dollars a year, but here in the Pirates' dugout, dragging on a cigarette, he seemed to be regarding the world warily. In 1978 Parker had been named the National League MVP, which led to the big contract. By the time of this photo, though, Parker's play had slipped a little bit, and his salary had become a source of fan resentment. It was, as they say, an unhealthy situation.

These days million-dollar salaries are commonplace in baseball, but smoking is a rarity, especially since cigarette-smoking manager Jim Leyland retired in 2013. That's a big change. For decades baseball teams had official cigarettes, and the list of stars who appeared in ads for them is startling: Babe Ruth, Joe DiMaggio, Ted Williams, Jackie Robinson, Willie Mays and Hank Aaron, for starters. At the time of this photo of Parker, smoking was already officially banned although players would occasionally transgress—the Mets' Keith Hernandez with his dugout drags famously among them. Overall though, it was the smokeless tobacco that had infiltrated dugouts that players preferred. Now baseball is attempting to quit that habit too. Since 2011 major league players have been prohibited from using or even carrying tobacco products while in uniform or at official team appearances. After the '14 death of Padres Hall of Famer Tony Gwynn from complications related to salivary gland cancer—Gwynn was just 54 and had been a long-time chaw man—baseball's 2016 labor agreement prohibited all new players entering the majors from using smokeless tobacco products. Many major league cities have also banned tobacco entirely from their stadiums. Let's call that a healthy situation.

Photograph by WALTER IOOSS JR.

FERNANDOMANIA

DODGER STADIUM, LOS ANGELES | *August 1, 1981*

AS PHENOMS GO, none have been more phenomenal
than Fernando Valenzeula. His hot start as a rookie in
1981 electrified two nations. He had been slated to be
the Dodgers' number 3 starter that year, but an injury
pushed Valenzuela to the mound on Opening Day. He
shut out the Houston Astros 2–0 on five hits and went
on to win his first eight starts, throwing complete games
in seven of them, with an ERA of 0.50. It was the most
dominant stretch of games by a pitcher since Bob Gibson
in '68. But the excitement of Fernandomania was about
much more than the results. Throwing the screwball,
looking skyward in mid-windup, the cherubic 20-year-
old moptop charmed—and captured imaginations.
Valenzuela helped the Dodgers set a major league home
attendance record and was a huge draw on the road.
He also had fans in Mexico excitedly on board, as they
followed the first major baseball star from their country.

From the time Walter O'Malley moved the Dodgers
from Brooklyn to Los Angeles after the 1957 season,
he had hoped for a Mexican star to broaden the team's
market. Now here was Fernando. Soon Dodgers games
were being televised in Mexico City, and the number of
radio stations in Mexico carrying those games jumped
from three to 17. In that '81 season, shortened by a labor
strike, Valenzuela became the first and still only pitcher
ever to win both the Rookie of the Year and Cy Young
Awards in the same year. He was an All-Star for his first
six seasons, going 21–11 in '86 with a majors-leading 20
complete games. But then the lefty's arm began to go.
Valenzuela pitched until '97, but he was often injured,
and no longer phenomenal. He did however still conjure
the spirit and memories of that phenomenal charm.

Photograph by ANDY HAYT

PURE HEAT

OLYMPIC STADIUM, MONTREAL | *April 27, 1983*

AFTER SETTING THE all-time strikeout record as an Astro on this day in 1983 (Montreal Expos infielder David Mills went down looking at a curveball), Nolan Ryan offered the analysis that "this will probably have to rate as my third-best record." At the top he placed his no-hitters mark—and that was when he only had five. In second place, he said, "I like 383 strikeouts in one season [1973, with the California Angels] because I did it without facing any pitchers." What he liked most about the career strikeouts record itself was that while Walter Johnson had struck out 3,509 in 21 seasons, Ryan needed only 16 seasons to overtake him. To Ryan, who missed few starts, this showed durability and persistence. If he had only known. Ryan, then 36, would pitch 10 more seasons, not losing much off a fastball that peaked at 101 miles per hour.

For a couple of years Ryan and Steve Carlton traded the strikeout record back and forth, but then Lefty suffered injuries and retired while the Ryan Express steamed ahead, leading the league in strikeouts four times in his 40s, extending the record to 5,714, which is 839 more than anyone else. Ryan threw his sixth no-hitter at the age of 43 and then at 44, a seventh, while striking out 16 batters. All told he took a no-hitter into the eighth inning 23 times. The marks against Ryan, such as they are, is that his won-loss record is not much above .500 (324–292) and he is also the all-time leader in bases on balls. Then again, he's among the leaders in inspiring awe among teammates as well. Said the Astros' Bob Knepper, "He just comes at you. You can't imagine how determined you have to be to throw your hardest fastball every time."

Photograph by MANNY MILLAN

SLOW RIDE

SHEA STADIUM, QUEENS, N.Y. | *August 26, 1983*

IT IS OFTEN the nature of technology that first we find out if we
are capable of creating something, and then we wonder whether
we need it. It was like that with the baseball cart. The early
adopters, if you will, were the Indians in 1950 and the White Sox
in '51. These versions were just cars—though the comedy potential
was tapped early when Chicago provided the visiting team with
a hearse to transport its relievers. The Milwaukee Braves tried a
chauffered Harley-Davidson scooter with the pitcher riding on a
sidecar. The first golf cart appeared in '63, with the L.A. Angels.
But like so much new technology, it didn't really go viral until the
design was perfected, and that happened in '67, when the Mets
introduced their take on the cart. That look—a baseball body topped
by a team cap—became the standard. By the '70s, just about every
team had one, and they became as much a visual signature of that
decade as wide collars and disco balls. Maybe the Mariners took it
too far. Seattle intended to haul its relievers out to the mound riding
a miniature fire boat (it looked like a tugboat). Reliever Jesse Orosco
(at right) would wind up coming in from the bullpen more than any
pitcher ever, and, pitching from 1979 to 2003, he bridged a cultural
divide. What was cool became uncool: Pitchers started running in
from the bullpen under their own power. Maybe a pro athlete being
dropped off at the mound like a kindergartner being taken to school
wasn't the greatest look after all. The carts disappeared—when the
Diamondbacks brought one back in '18, few pitchers used it—but
the charms of the object remain. In '15 the original Mets cart came
up for auction at Sotheby's, and while the estimate was that it might
fetch $20,000, it sold for $112,500. Beauty is never obsolete.

Photograph by JOHN IACONO

TOO GOOD TO BE TRUE

BEACH, ST. PETERSBURG, FLORIDA | *March 18, 1985*

THE SUB-HEADLINE OF the SPORTS ILLUSTRATED story about the Mets' sensational new prospect Hayden Siddhartha (Sidd) Finch hinted that he was more than just another prospect: "He's a pitcher, part yogi and part recluse. Impressively liberated from our opulent lifestyle, Sidd's deciding about yoga—and his future in baseball." Finch's fastball, wrote George Plimpton in that story, had been clocked at an unprecedented 168 miles per hour. But there was a catch: The pitcher was torn between baseball and pursuing his other passion, the French horn. Furthermore he was a Harvard dropout who spoke 10 languages and he threw with one foot bare and the other in a boot. He was 6'4" and had been raised by monks. To be honest, there was an even bigger catch. The Finch story's issue date was April 1, 1985. More to the point, the letters of the first words of the subhead spelled out HAPPY APRIL FOOLS DAY.

The Mets helped with the prank, giving photographer Lane Stewart access to their spring training facilities. In the story Mets players John Christensen, Dave Cochrane and Lenny Dykstra are shown peeking through a flap into the secret enclosure where Finch liked to throw, and catcher Ronn Reynolds posed for a photo featuring his supposedly aching hands. This was 1985, long before email and social media, and for days many readers believed Finch was real. The joke resonated so deeply that the man who posed as Finch in the photos—a friend of Stewart's, middle school art teacher Joe Berton—continued to be recognized 25 years later. A happy coda for Mets fans whose brief excitement about Finch had been dashed: Next season their team won the World Series all on their own, without Finch's ever taking the mound.

Photograph by LANE STEWART

> "Carew has an uncanny ability to move the ball around as if the bat were some kind of magic wand."
> —**KEN HOLTZMAN**, PITCHER

NO SWEETER STROKE

ANAHEIM STADIUM, ANAHEIM | *August 4, 1985*

THE HITTER WHO provided the most consistent threat to batting .400 since Ted Williams actually did it learned baseball playing with a broom handle and tennis balls in his native Panama. Rod Carew—born on a moving train and named after the man who delivered him, Dr. Rodney Cline—didn't even play high school baseball upon moving to New York City with his family at age 15. But Carew did find games in his neighborhood park, where he caught the eye of a Minnesota Twins scout, and the team signed him after a 1964 tryout. In '67 Carew won Rookie of the Year with a respectable .292 batting average. In his third season he adjusted his stance, lowering himself into a deeper crouch, and he became the superior batsman of his time. Standing less upright was the key adjustment, but Carew's ability to fine-tune not just on off-days or during the course of a game but in the middle of at bats made him a tough puzzle at the plate. Over the years other batters made runs at .400—George Brett, Tony Gwynn—but Carew tantalized several times, carrying plus-.400 averages through mid-June in '74 and '75, and into July in '83. In '77, his best season, Carew was hitting .401 on July 10 before his numbers settled. So all he ended up with that year was the American League MVP award and a .388 average (50 points ahead of the majors' next best). That batting title was one of seven for Carew, which, when he retired, was the most for any player since Ty Cobb. Carew went into the Hall of Fame as a Minnesota Twin, but he closed out his career with the Angels for whom he got his 3,000th hit—a Carew-classic opposite-field single, against the Twins no less—in the photo at right.

Photograph by V.J. LOVERO

153

THE WIZARD

BUSCH STADIUM, ST. LOUIS | *October 12, 1985*

AS A KID growing up in the Watts section of Los Angeles, Ozzie Smith and his friends entertained themselves by going to the neighborhood lumberyard and doing flips off tires onto piles of sawdust. As a baseball player, flips were still good fun. He first did them in spring training and then, as a rookie in 1978, Smith followed a suggestion by teammate Gene Tenace and did a backflip when he took the field for Fan Appreciation Day, the last game of the season. A tradition was born. In San Diego and then, starting in '82, after he was traded to the Cardinals, in St. Louis, Smith began the first and last games of each season by doing a backflip as he ran out to play shortstop—and he did it during the postseason as well. The backflip resonated because it reflected not only Smith's ball-field joy, but also the manner in which he played his position: like an acrobat. Teammates recall in awe the time he ran back after a bloop fly, leaped for the ball and, realizing in mid-air he needed to avoid oncoming leftfielder Curt Ford, contorted his body and made the catch. That athletic ability gave Smith his historically wide range.

"If he misses a ball," the Mets' Bud Harrelson once said, "you assume it's uncatchable." The Wizard of Oz won 13 straight Gold Gloves from 1980 to '92, saving runs and games like no shortstop before or since, and his nimble glove (plus 2,460 hits and 580 steals) got him to Hall of Fame. In 1995, at the age of 40, Smith took the field at Busch Stadium on Opening Day and the way he came flipping across the infield, the message was unmistakable. Spring is here.

Photograph by RICH PILLING

THE ART OF THE CRAFT

CLEARWATER, FLORIDA | *March 20, 1986*

SO TED WILLIAMS and Wade Boggs and Don Mattingly walk into a restaurant. It is spring training, 1986, and the restaurant is Tio Pepe in Clearwater, Fla. Williams and Boggs had come from Winter Haven, where the Red Sox were training (and Williams worked as an instructor, advising Boggs among others). Mattingly, coming off an MVP season with the Yankees, arrived from Sarasota. SI's Peter Gammons had invited these lefty legends to talk hitting and to debate the virtues of Williams's method compared to that of Charley Lau's, whose teachings influenced both Boggs and Mattingly. After a sometimes contentious debate about the merits of Williams's unlocking the hips versus Lau's shifting one's weight, Gammons pointed out that the differences were largely semantic. Then the three hitters started shooting the breeze. For instance, did they always stand in the same place in the batter's box? Boggs, yes; Mattingly, no: He would move in on pitchers he believed he could attack; Williams said he moved in on pitchers who threw down and away because, "I never wanted to let that nibbler get me out." The most curious detail: Williams asked Mattingly if he'd ever smelled burning wood when a fastball's seams contacted his bat just right. For Williams, it happened five or six times in his career. Mattingly said he had smelled the burn two or three times. Boggs announced, "I thought I'd heard everything about hitting, but that's unbelievable."

Photograph by RONALD C. MODRA

WITHIN THE WALL

FENWAY PARK, BOSTON | *June 21, 1987*

AS PART OF a wide-ranging SPORTS ILLUSTRATED cover story titled, ONE DAY IN BASEBALL, writer E.M. Swift spent an afternoon behind the manually operated scoreboard at Boston's Fenway Park. Fenway, which opened in 1912, still has a scoreboard in which human beings physically keep track of the score, specifically with 12-by-16-inch metal plates with numbers on them. That scoreboard—which is located inside the tall leftfield wall, the Green Monster—is but one element of the park's idiosyncratic charm. (The rightfield wall checking in at three-feet tall, or 34 feet shorter than the Monster, is among the delights.) During his time behind the scoreboard, Swift also discovered some of the less charming aspects of Fenway's rustic nature. For instance the operators, Bill Rose, 31 *(in the foreground of the photo)* and James Stokes, 19, blared a radio in order to scare away rats. Swift described the bathroom facilities as a "chamber pot." No refreshments are available to the scoreboard operators. Still, their job had plentiful upside. Peering through slats in the walls, Rose and Stokes enjoyed an immersive view, following the action from where a leftfielder might stand in a ballpark of typical dimensions. Line drives rattled the workplace. In later years, Manny Ramirez arrived in Boston and added still greater joy for operators. The chimerical Sox slugger—who played leftfield at Fenway for eight All-Star seasons—was known to pop into the wall, mid-inning to wait out a pitching change, talking or browsing the web and usually, although not always, getting back out to his position by the time the game was set to resume.

Photograph by WALTER IOOSS JR.

GENERATION TO GENERATION

RIVERFRONT STADIUM, CINCINNATI | *July 12, 1989*

BASEBALL BEGINS FOR so many with a ball tossed from parent to child, or with games watched as a family. So it was naturally a big story when Ken Griffey Sr. and Ken Griffey Jr. became the first father and son to play in the majors at the time, in 1989, the father with the Cincinnati Reds and the son with the Seattle Mariners. At the time of this photo Griffey Sr. was 39, his son 19. Ken Griffey Sr. was a three-time All-Star who had been a vital part of Cincinnati's Big Red Machine teams in the '70s. His son was on an even higher trajectory, a No. 1 overall draft pick who 27 years later, in 2016, would be voted into the Hall of Fame by the highest margin (99.32%) of any player ever. It turned out that merely being in the same major league wasn't enough for the father and son. In 1990 Griffey Sr. engineered a move to Seattle, putting the duo on the same team, where they sat together in the dugout. Imaginations were officially captured.

In Griffey Sr.'s first game as a Mariner, on Aug. 31, the two followed each other in the lineup, with dad batting second and his son third. They each hit singles in their first at bats, and both came around to score. Afterward Senior, owner of two World Series rings, declared, "This is the best thing that's ever happened to me." In a game two weeks later the father and son hit back-to-back home runs. In his 88 plate appearances with Seattle that year, Griffey Sr. batted .377 with three home runs, a notable improvement on his numbers with the Reds earlier that season, when he hit .206 with one homer in 68 plate appearances. Nothing gets a man on his toes like wanting to show his boy how it's done.

Photograph by RONALD C. MODRA

QUAKING

CANDLESTICK PARK, SAN FRANCISCO | *October 19, 1989*

THE BIGGEST EARTHQUAKE to hit the Bay Area since 1906 happened to arrive at 5:04 p.m. on Oct. 17, about 30 minutes before the two local teams, the Oakland A's and San Francisco Giants, were to take the field for Game 3 of the World Series. "We're having an . . . " began television announcer Al Michaels, doing pregame coverage from a shaking Candlestick Park, and before he could complete his sentence the power went out. The quake registered 6.9 on the Richter scale. Candlestick, which opened in 1960, withstood the 20 seconds of tremors with minimal harm, after which some relieved fans shouted "Play ball!" But elsewhere the Bay Area was hit hard. A section of the upper deck of the Bay Bridge collapsed onto the lower deck, and part of Oakland's Nimitz Freeway also fell. Sixty-three people died, and nearly 4,000 were injured.

Some speculated that the World Series actually saved lives because people were home to watch the game, making the roadways less crowded. Baseball commissioner Fay Vincent, after considering moving the Series to another location or canceling it altogether, elected to postpone play while the recovery work began. This photo shows workmen repairing damage to the upper deck in Candlestick Park. On Oct. 27 the Series resumed in San Francisco, and Oakland, which had been up two games to none completed the sweep. After winning Game 4 the A's opted for a relatively quiet celebration, deciding that, given all that had happened, it wasn't the right time for players to start dousing each other with champagne.

Photograph by BETTMANN/GETTY IMAGES

UNDAUNTED

MUNICIPAL STADIUM, CLEVELAND | *May 11, 1991*

JIM ABBOTT WAS BORN with no right hand, which in a way, he has said, was a key to his success—not the absence of the hand, but the timing. If he had lost the hand later in life, learning the particular mechanics of his situation might have seemed too daunting. But playing baseball with one hand was all he knew, so he went with it— all the way to the majors. The deftness with which Abbott managed his disability was most evident in his fielding. The 6' 3", 200-pound southpaw was so quick in switching the glove from the end of his right arm, where he would perch it while throwing a pitch, onto his left hand, that he was able to snare comeback grounders to the mound. As he advanced through youth baseball, many doubted he could continue at the next level. But at the University of Michigan, Abbott was named best amateur player in the country, and in 1988 he played for the U.S. Olympic team, pitching a complete game win in the gold medal final against Japan.

In 1989 Abbott made the starting rotation of the California Angels, and two years later he went 18–11 with a 2.89 ERA and finished third in the Cy Young voting. His crowning achievement came in '93 when as a member of the Yankees he pitched a no-hitter against the Indians. After the final out his teammates mobbed the mound and Abbott high-fived every one of them with that powerful left arm. After his 10 seasons in the majors Abbott became a motivational speaker, a second career that may have been inevitable, given all the inspiration provided in his first.

Photograph by DAVID LIAM KYLE

"Every year in spring training, I talk to the
[Royals'] minor leaguers . . . there's always some
18-year-old kid out of high school [who says],
'Hey, tell me about the pine tar game.' "
—GEORGE BRETT

A STICKY SITUATION

MUNICIPAL STADIUM, CLEVELAND | *August 4, 1991*

GEORGE BRETT, THE Hall of Fame third baseman for the Kansas City Royals, was unusual in that he never wore batting gloves. He relied on pine tar for a better grip, applying it liberally to his bats as he is doing here, near the end of his 21-year career, just a few months removed from winning his third batting title. Brett stuck with his pine tar to the end, even though, eight years before this photo was taken, that glutinous practice became an issue. It was July of 1983 and the Royals were playing their then-rivals at Yankee Stadium. With two outs in the ninth inning Brett hit a two-run home run off Goose Gossage to put Kansas City ahead 5–4. In an earlier series the Yankees had noticed that Brett's pine tar went higher up the bat than the 18 inches allowed by rule, and they had been waiting for the perfect moment to raise the issue. This was it. Manager Billy Martin asked the umpires to check Brett's bat. Brett remembers that the day was hot and his hands had been sweaty so he had generously applied the pine tar, and that this was a bat he had been treating between every at bat for weeks. The umpire crew huddled and, for visual emphasis, set the bat down across the width of home plate (17 inches). Then umpire Tim McClelland turned toward the Royals dugout and, with a pump of the forearm, called Brett out. His home run was erased. Brett charged instantly and urgently, hair flying, arms flailing, eyes wide and left cheek bulging. Gossage said, "I have never seen anyone as mad as George Brett on that day." After the game, won 4–3 by New York, the Royals lodged a protest with the league that was upheld, invoking the "spirit of the rules." The final inning was restarted before the team's next meeting, with Brett still tossed out. Kansas City won 5–4.

Photograph by DAVID LIAM KYLE

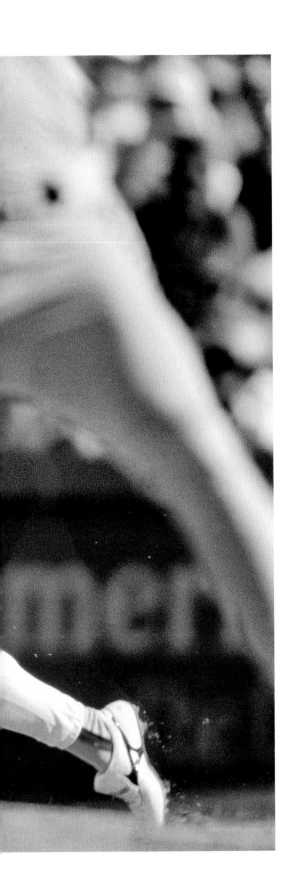

SEE RICKEY RUN

OAKLAND COLISEUM, OAKLAND | *October 11, 1992*

AS A HIGH SCHOOL football player in Oakland, Rickey Henderson made the all-city team at both running back and linebacker. He wanted to play pro football, but his mother, worried about career-ending injuries, steered her son toward baseball. On the diamond, Henderson still showed a running back's knack for bursting through an opening in the defense. Head down, legs churning, he set records for stolen bases in a season (130 in 1982) and a career (1,406). He had technical skill too. From his batter's crouch he set the record for unintentional walks, which is amazing, because the pitcher knew that if gave Henderson first base, it was likely that he would be on second before the next batter had taken a swing. But then, you *had* to pitch carefully to Henderson; he hit 297 career home runs, including a record 81 to lead off a game. He was, simply, the most disruptive leadoff hitter ever. As Oakland A's teammate Mitchell Page put it, "Rickey Henderson is a run."

To be accurate, he was 2,295 runs, another record. His personality was not for everyone. Rickey often referred to himself as Rickey. And after setting the career stolen base record, he crowed "Lou Brock is the symbol of great basestealing, but today I am the greatest of all time" while Brock, who had just presented Henderson with a plaque, stood beside him. But Henderson loved the game enough to play it for 25 seasons with nine teams, among them the Padres, whom he came to as a free agent after phoning San Diego general manager Kevin Towers and saying: "This is Rickey calling on behalf of Rickey. Rickey wants to play baseball."

Photograph by V.J. LOVERO

KING GEORGE

PADDOCK, OCALA, FLORIDA | *February 15, 1993*

GEORGE STEINBRENNER NEEDED no coaxing to don a Napoleon costume for a SPORTS ILLUSTRATED cover story that ran in March 1993. The occasion was his return to baseball after being banned for 2½ years, for paying gambler Howard Spira $40,000 to supply dirt on Dave Winfield, one of his players. The Napoleon outfit was suggested after Steinbrenner had been making comparisons to the French emperor's return from exile. Clearly this was a man who greatly enjoyed the fame, and power, of being the Yankees' owner. Steinbrenner, a shipbuilding heir, bought into the team as principal owner in '73, and soon slid into the role of big-spending villain for baseball's free-agency era. With local television money to back him up, The Boss opened his wallet for stars such as Catfish Hunter, Reggie Jackson, Winfield, Jason Giambi, Alex Rodriguez and more. When he wasn't handing out rich contracts, he was firing managers with historic frequency. He fired Yogi Berra 16 games into a season. He fired Bob Lemon 14 games into a season. He hired Billy Martin five times. In the '50s Steinbrenner had been an assistant football coach at Northwestern and Purdue, and as owner he was not afraid to let his authoritarian streak show. While he had many detractors, Steinbrenner delivered results. His teams appeared in 11 World Series, winning seven. His Yankees also started their own TV network, YES, an innovation followed by other teams and conferences. When he was portrayed on the sitcom *Seinfeld* as an off-kilter despot, he was able to laugh about it and even agreed to play himself in one episode, never one to shy from the spotlight.

Photograph by BILL FRAKES

THE ARMS OF ATLANTA

MUNICIPAL STADIUM, WEST PALM BEACH, FLORIDA | *February 21, 1993*

THE BRAVES HAD already competed in the World Series in 1991 and '92, losing both times, when Atlanta signed Greg Maddux before the '93 season. Maddux had won a Cy Young Award with the Chicago Cubs the previous year, and when he joined a rotation that already included Tom Glavine and John Smoltz (as well as the eminently competent Steve Avery and Pete Smith) the feeling was heady. "Barring a trade, we're going to be together for at least four years," Smoltz said of the starters, boldly adding. "The Braves don't want to create a team that wins one World Series and then sees everybody jump ship." Indeed the Big Three at least stayed on board somewhat longer than four years—until 2002 in fact—and in one sense everything went as imagined. In all the Braves won 14 consecutive division titles (excepting the strike year of '94) a run of success unparalleled in baseball history. And the three stars shone brightly. Glavine *(front in the photo)* won a Cy Young in '98 and produced five 20-win seasons. Maddux *(behind Glavine)* won three consecutive Cy Young Awards, from 1993 to '95, and led the majors in ERA four times. Smoltz *(above Smith and below Avery)* had a Cy Young campaign as a starter in '96, and then, pitching out of the bullpen in 2002, he led the majors with 55 saves. All three are enshrined in the Hall of Fame. The fly in the ointment: With all those playoff chances, the Braves won only one World Series, against the Cleveland Indians in 1995. Thus was proven a baseball adage. Over the long haul of a 162-game season, starting pitching can carry you. In a short series, anything can happen.

Photograph by RONALD C. MODRA

"Touch 'em all Joe. You'll never hit a
bigger home run in your life."
—**TOM CHEEK**, BLUE JAYS RADIO ANNOUNCER

NORTHERN EXPOSURE

SKYDOME, TORONTO | *October 23, 1993*

YOU COULD ARGUE that Joe Carter's home run in the bottom
of the ninth in Game 6 of the 1993 World Series was the most
dramatic walk-off home run in baseball history. Carter clinched
the entire Series, unlike Kirk Gibson in Game 1 in '88. And while
Bill Mazeroski's solo shot in 1960 came in a tie game, Carter hit
his three-run homer with his team trailing by a run, with one out
and two on. If Carter hits a grounder, his team is done. Agree with
this analysis, or don't agree. But one distinctive aspect of Carter's
home run is beyond argument: It was enjoyed most deeply by fans
outside the United States, and that was historic.

Major League baseball first expanded to Canada in 1969, in
Montreal, but the Expos made the playoffs only once, losing to the
Dodgers in '81, before moving to Washington, D.C., in 2005 and
becoming the Nationals. The Toronto Blue Jays began play as an
expansion team in 1977 and won their first World Series in '92,
over the Atlanta Braves. That year Carter, at first base, had the
honor of recording the final out, in the 11th inning of a Game 6,
and the clubhouse celebrants included hockey great Wayne
Gretzky. In Game 6 of the '93 Series, Carter came to the plate
with his team down 6–5, facing Philadelphia Phillies closer Mitch
"Wild Thing" Williams, who had already blown a lead in Game 4.
Carter blasted a Williams fastball over the leftfield wall and into
the Blue Jays' bullpen, and then he hopped around the bases and
into the arms of his exultant teammates as fireworks went off. For
America's pastime, it was a Canadian high point.

Photograph by WILLIAM R. SMITH

1994
to
2018

Florida Marlins' World Series ring, 1997

Wildness

JORDAN ON THE FARM

HOOVER METROPOLITAN STADIUM, BIRMINGHAM, ALABAMA | *July 14, 1994*

MICHAEL JORDAN HAD just thrown out the ceremonial first pitch at a 1993 Chicago White Sox playoff game when rumors filled the park that the Chicago Bulls shooting guard, after winning three consecutive NBA titles, would retire from basketball at age 30. Jordan confirmed the news the following morning, and at the time his next move was unknown. Then in February he signed a minor league contract with those same White Sox, who, like the Bulls, were owned by Jerry Reinsdorf. Some speculated that Jordan's choice was motivated by the July '93 murder of his father James, who had played semipro baseball. Others thought Jordan might be ducking a suspension, with the NBA investigating his gambling activities. Jordan offered a simpler explanation: He loved baseball, which he had played as a teenager in North Carolina at Laney High. Jordan wore 45, his old high school number, went to spring training with the big league club, and was assigned to the White

Sox Double A affiliate Birmingham Barons, managed by Terry Francona. He brought in a luxury bus so his team could meet its Southern League appointments in comfort, and the Barons enjoyed record attendance. But the 6' 6" outfielder, who once called the ump a ref, had his struggles. Jordan struck out in more than a quarter of his 436 at bats, and he batted just .202. His experiment seemed to confirm that even an elite athlete who works extremely hard at baseball (as Jordan did) can not simply take up the game at a professional level. Baseball is too hard. Jordan did, however, show some promise with a 13-game hitting streak, 30 stolen bases and 51 RBIs, and he said he would have continued with baseball if not for the labor strike that ran into the following season. Instead of sitting out or crossing a picket line, the best basketball player in the world returned to the hardwood.

Photograph by PATRICK MURPHY-RACEY

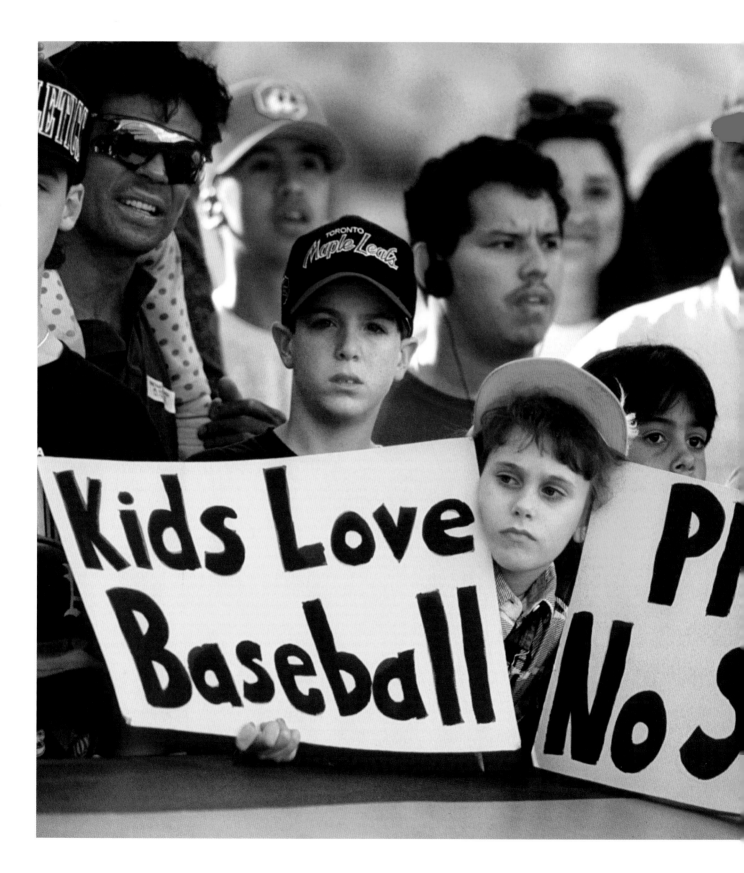

FORSAKING THE FAITHFUL

OAKLAND COLISEUM, OAKLAND | *August 11, 1994*

THE PROMISE OF every sports season is that it will end in the crowning of a champion. That promise was broken, for the first time in any sport, with the baseball strike of 1994. Baseball had seen seven previous work stoppages, including a nasty one in '81 that cut out the middle of the season and resulted in the oddity of sending first-half and second-half champs to the playoffs (while the Cincinnati Reds, owner of the best overall record in the National League, stayed home because they hadn't won their division in either half). But the '94 strike was worse. The owners wanted to impose a salary cap, and the union, led by Donald Fehr, wouldn't go for it. So the games stopped on Aug. 12—the day after these fans pleaded for mercy at a Mariners-A's game—and didn't resume. No playoffs, no World Series. Lost in the work stoppage were dramas such as Tony Gwynn's run at .400 (he was at .394 when the players struck) and Matt Williams's chance to surpass Roger Maris's single-season home run mark. (Williams had 43 before the strike wiped out his Giants' final 47 games.) The '94 strike may have been most painful to fans in Montreal. The Expos had baseball's best record at 74–40 when the curtain went down. Imagine the frustration of rooting for a team that had never won a postseason series, and the year they're really good, baseball cancels its playoffs. Fans around the league were so disgusted that in 1995 (a strike-shortened, 144-game schedule began on April 25) average attendance was down 20%. The one positive of the strike was that it was such a disaster both sides may have learned something: Baseball hasn't had a work stoppage since.

Photograph by OTTO GREULE JR/GETTY IMAGES

WAITING FOR SHOW TIME

THE BALLPARK IN ARLINGTON, ARLINGTON, TEXAS | *May 20, 1995*

NAME ANY PLAYER. How about Jose Oquendo? Sure. Now come up another player whose first name begins with the first letter of Oquendo's last name. Oscar Gamble. Now keep it going like that. Giancarlo Stanton. Shawon Dunston. Dave Kingman. Kyle Seager. Sam Rice and so on. Play the name game for a few hours every day from April to October and you'll have an idea of what it is like to spend a season as a relief pitcher in the bullpen. You have time to kill as you wait to be called in. Look at the faces of the Brewers relievers in this photo. They could be in the backseat for a long car trip, wondering, "Are we there yet?" The name game is a common distraction, but those consigned to the bullpen have many others. For many years the Mets maintained a vegetable garden—tomatoes, squash, radishes—in their bullpen at Shea Stadium. From 1998 to 2013, the Diamondbacks had a bullpen catcher, Jeff Motuzas, who would entertain the bored pitchers by eating improbable things for a fee: a bowl of horseradish, say, or a dozen glazed doughnuts. These days Baltimore Orioles relievers clap together to mark the number of runs their team has scored. Anything to change the pace.

Relief pitchers have gotten in on the action a bit more over time. In the 1967 season for example, relievers pitched an average of 2.61 innings per game. In 2017, 50 years later, it was 3.19 innings per game. Still, there remains plenty of time to fill and rain delays only increase the need for amusement. In 2017 the bullpens at Wrigley Field in Chicago were moved from the sidelines of the field to below the bleachers and gave the pitchers from the home and opposing teams the ability to interact through monitors. During a rain delay at a Diamondbacks-Cubs game that year, the bullpens exchanged visual gags—donning animal masks, lining up chairs and pretending to be on a bobsled, engaging in human bowling. These routines and others like them help give the expression "staying loose in the bullpen" a whole new meaning.

Photograph by DAVID WOO

> "He pitches. He's not a thrower. He sank the ball, ran it away from hitters, took a little bit off his fastball and still reached back for something extra when he needed to."
> —**JOE GIRARDI**, CUBS CATCHER

HEIGHT OF SUCCESS

KINGDOME, SEATTLE | *June 14, 1995*

BEING 6' 10" WAS not always an advantage, according to Randy Johnson. He suggested that shorter pitchers have less body to control, and said: "For me it was difficult because I was so tall." The Big Unit made that remark after learning that he was being inducted into the Baseball Hall of Fame, so obviously he got a handle on the height issue. But it took a while. Johnson, who attended USC on a joint scholarship for basketball and baseball, could throw a 102 mph fastball but struggled with control as a young pitcher, leading the majors in walks three years in a row. When he turned 29, he had a career won-loss record of 48–45. But during an offseason throwing session Nolan Ryan offered a tip about Johnson's foot placement during delivery, and Johnson began to harness his power and become baseball's most intimidating pitcher. In 1995, as a Seattle Mariner, he won his first Cy Young Award. With Arizona he won four consecutive Cy Youngs from 1999 to 2002, and had a 3–0 record as the Diamondbacks beat the Yankees in the 2001 World Series. He finished his career with 303 wins and only 166 losses, and his strikeout rate per nine innings (10.6) is the best in history. His on-field persona might be defined by two memorable moments. At the '93 All-Star Game, he sailed a first pitch over the head of lefthanded batter John Kruk, who for the rest of the at bat made a comic show of staying out of Johnson's way. Then there was that poor bird. In a 2001 spring training game Johnson's pitch hit a dove in flight and it appeared to be vaporized, feathers flying, in one of baseball's early viral videos. The collision was dumb luck—terrible for the bird, of course, but another image to remind batters just what they were up against.

Photograph by RICH FRISHMAN

PHANS DELIGHT

VETERANS STADIUM, PHILADELPHIA | *July 2, 1995*

THE RESEMBLANCE BETWEEN the Phillie Phanatic and a Muppet is not a coincidence: The mascot was created in Jim Henson's puppet factory. And like Kermit the Frog and Fozzie Bear, the Phanatic, even in his mascot's silence, has been entertaining families for generations. Costumed mascots have enlivened baseball since Mr. Met arrived in 1964, and he helped amuse fans through long and losing seasons. By now all but three big league teams have a mascot, and Mr. Met has a wife (above, the couple is hosting friends at the 2013 All-Star Game). The Phanatic, introduced in '78, is one of the most popular in the game, and the extent to which he took off in Philadelphia was unexpected. At the time of his creation the Phillies were offered the copyright to the character for an extra $1,300 and turned it down. A few years later the Phanatic was a bona fide star and the team bought the copyright—for $250,000. For 16 seasons the Phanatic was played by Dave Raymond, who was tapped for the job while a student intern and who possessed a gift for nonverbal communication he attributed to being raised by a deaf mother. The Phanatic became the best kind of stadium hero—one who never gets injured, goes into a slump or leaves in free agency.

The Phanatic does his best work in dugout dances, hexing visiting pitchers and generally taunting members of the opposing team, such as the fallen Atlanta Brave at left. His craziest day occurred during the summer of 1988 when he was clowning with a blow-up doll dressed in a Tommy Lasorda jersey (with overstuffed belly). The Dodgers manager came out of the dugout and, with no humor and little restraint, hit the Phanatic with the doll, nearly knocking off the mascot's head. Mascots, now ubiquitous across sports, were at the forefront of changing times at the ballpark—as game action became augmented with kiss cams, theme nights and T-shirt cannons. The players are the stars of the Show, but mascots are the ringleaders of the circus.

Photographs by JOHN IACONO *(left) and* MARK CUNNINGHAM/MLB PHOTOS/GETTY IMAGES

IRON MAN

CAMDEN YARDS, BALTIMORE | *September 6, 1995*

CAL RIPKEN JR. WAS done with the moment. He sat in the dugout, ready for the game to resume. The cheers had gone on for 10 full minutes as he had shared the accomplishment with his family and endured seven curtain calls, with the banner on the warehouse beyond the outfield wall having flipped from 2130 to 2131. But the fans kept cheering "We Want Cal!" They would not stop. The occasion of Ripken's breaking the once unfathomable consecutive games record held by Lou Gehrig was not something the people in the park were ready to let go of. And so, aided by shoves from Orioles teammates Rafael Palmeiro and Bobby Bonilla, Ripken emerged from the dugout and began trotting up the first base line, high-fiving, shaking hands. Soon he was doing a full-fledged victory lap of the stadium, greeting fans, grounds crew, police officers, even the visiting California Angels players. He touched 'em all. "After one handshake, two handshakes, two looks in the face, all of a sudden it became a whole lot more intimate of a celebration," Ripken said. "It didn't matter anymore how long the delay was going to be, I'm going to enjoy this." Camden Yards was stocked with luminaries (President Bill Clinton, Joe DiMaggio, Brooks Robinson, Frank Robinson), and coming the year after the World Series had been canceled by a player's strike, this 22-minute game delay was a moment for fans to celebrate the virtue of showing up for work. Ripken's streak began on May 30, 1982 and ended on Sept. 19, 1998, 2,632 games later. He was an All-Star shortstop in the last 16 of those 17 seasons, and, as a matter of interest, over the two games in which he tied and then broke Gehrig's record, he had five hits and hit a home run in each. Ripken, doing his job.

Photograph by WALTER IOOSS JR.

THE MAGIC OF THE MOVIES

FARM, DYERSVILLE, IOWA | *June 22, 1997*

THE BEST BASEBALL movies have made lasting contributions to the game's cultural life. When a not-even-close pitch is described as "juuust a bit outside," it's a callback to Bob Uecker's goofy announcer character in the comedy *Major League* (1989). Any mound conference that goes on too long becomes a reference to *Bull Durham* ('88), where the talk on the hill turned to wedding presents, and offered the timeless wisdom, "candlesticks always make a nice gift." *A League of Their Own* ('92) gave us "there's no crying in baseball." From *The Pride of the Yankees* ('42) to *The Bad News Bears* ('76) to *Moneyball* (2011), the game has had a rich life on screen, and no movie celebrated baseball's allure quite like *Field of Dreams* (1989). The movie's signature line, "If you build it, he will come," is also its plot engine: That command inspires Ray Kinsella to build a baseball diamond in his Iowa cornfield. Soon Shoeless Joe Jackson and other players from the 1919 Black Sox emerge from the stalks to play ball. The field becomes a place to grasp at lost opportunities, culminating with Ray's finding one more chance to toss the ball around with his dad. At the end the movie's writer character, Terence Mann, waxes about the magnetic attraction of baseball and urges Ray to keep his diamond, "This field, this game: It's a part of our past, Ray. It reminds us of all that once was good and could be again. Oh . . . people will come, Ray. People will most definitely come." They came in the movie, and in real life too, to the film-set field in Dyersville, Iowa, where the reenactment pictured at left took place, and where visitors arrive hoping to feel some of that celluloid spirit themselves.

Photograph by CHARLIE NEIBERGALL/AP/SHUTTERSTOCK

AS GOOD AS IT GETS

JOHNNY ROSENBLATT STADIUM, OMAHA | *June 17, 2000*

COLLEGE BASEBALL'S WORLD SERIES occupies a funny, in-between place in the baseball firmament. It doesn't have quite the stubble-free, playing-house charm of the Little League World Series. Nor does it feel like an under-23 version of the major league World Series, because baseball's greatest prodigies, from Mickey Mantle to Mike Trout (and countless more), sign contracts out of high school. College baseball can be a road to the majors for some but it is not necessarily the fastest or the highest profile one.

Still, the sport can draw a crowd. College World Series games, played since 1950 on a neutral site in Omaha, regularly attract more than 20,000 fans. They come to see schools such as LSU, a powerhouse that's won six NCAA titles. The Tigers team that won it all in 2000 had its share of future big leaguers—among them Brad Hawpe, who became an All-Star outfielder with the Rockies— yet the players who were the force behind the celebration in this photo were not big league bound. This was their shining moment and here's what happened: LSU trailed top-ranked Stanford 5–2 in the eighth inning of the winner-take-all final. Then home runs by Blair Barbier and Jeremy Witten tied the game. In the bottom of the ninth LSU had runners on first and second when Brad Cresse came to the plate. That year Cresse won the Johnny Bench Award as the nation's most outstanding collegiate catcher, and he would go on to play in the minors for seven seasons without ever getting the call-up. Here in the ninth, Cresse singled to leftfield, the winning run scored, and then, for LSU, some kind of ecstatic joy—big-time, major-league joy—ensued.

Photograph by DAMIAN STROHMEYER

EVERY BREATH HE TAKES . . .

LEGENDS FIELD, TAMPA | *February 23, 2003*

WHEN HIDEKI MATSUI, a huge star from Japan's Nippon league, signed with the New York Yankees in December of 2002, reporters in two countries rushed to file stories. More than 400 media members attended Matsui's introductory press conference at a Manhattan hotel, and once the games began, the chronicling of Matsui took on even greater urgency—even during spring training, as seen at left. On a typical day at the ballpark, the leftfielder and designated hitter might have had 80 media members from Japan there to track his at bats. Their reports were more concerned with those results, and with issues such as how Matsui was faring in the United States than with whether the Yankees won or lost. This phenomenon was first observed in 1995, when pitcher Hideo Nomo came to the Dodgers from Japan and put together a season that led him to be named National League Rookie of the Year. Since then dedicated media folks have obsessively followed such imports as Ichiro Suzuki (who began his MLB career with the Mariners), Daisuke Matsuzaka (Red Sox) and Shohei Ohtani (Angels). When Ohtani made his pitching debut in Oakland in 2018, 240 credentialed media members from Japan documented the moment.

When Matsui came to New York, the Yankees hired Isao Hirooka, a former sportswriter in Tokyo, to help manage and corral the throng of media. According to Hirooka, Matsui worried that Japanese reporters would be a bother to his teammates and the Yankees' regular beat writers. So that crew was kept to a restricted area, and Matsui talked to them every day. Unlike most other media, their job was straightforward: No need to chase the player of the moment. They always knew where their story was.

Photograph by NEW YORK YANKEES

A HOMELAND OF DREAMS

SAN PEDRO DE MACORIS, DOMINICAN REPUBLIC | *July 31, 2003*

LOOK AT THE KID in the far right of the photo, scaling the baseball field wall. Maybe he's going up to sit on the wall and watch beside his friends, or maybe he is planning to drop down on the other side. Whatever his aim, he's pursuing it doggedly. Welcome to baseball in the Dominican Republic, where enthusiasm for the game runs strong—in some cases, desperately so. Nearly a third of the island lives in poverty, and many boys view the game their best shot at the good life. Juan Marichal was a rarity at the time he became baseball's first Dominican-born star, dominating for the Giants in the 1960s. Now Dominicans are a major force. In 2018, more major league players born outside the U.S. came from the Dominican Republic than from any other country, and teams have invested in cultivating that pipeline. In 1987 the Los Angeles Dodgers became the first club to establish a formal training academy on the island. The academy, focusing on players in their late teens, helped the Dodgers sign and develop outstanding talents such as Pedro Martinez, Raul Mondesi and Adrian Beltre. Now all 30 teams have academies there, and Major League Baseball maintains its own office in the Dominican Republic. But for every Vladimir Guerrero or David Ortiz who graduates to big ballparks and major league money, many more are obviously left behind. An estimated 3% of the Dominican players who are signed make it to the big leagues, and many young players have their first bonuses siphoned away by unscrupulous street agents. And yet, the dream of the big leagues, combined with a deep-running passion for the game, keeps those kids swinging, and climbing.

Photograph by JOE CAVARETTA/AP

REACHING OUT, TOUCHING YOU

WRIGLEY FIELD, CHICAGO | *October 14, 2003*

IF BASEBALL'S GOATS had a Hall of Fame, the inaugural class would surely include Fred Merkle (Giants, 1908), Don Denkinger ('85 World Series umpire), Bill Buckner (Red Sox '86) and Steve Bartman, a mere fan who had no idea when he took his seat along the leftfield line at Wrigley Field for Game 6 of the 2003 National League Championship Series between the Cubs and the Marlins that he would emerge as the game's central character. In the eighth inning, the Cubs, ahead in the series three games to two, led the Marlins 3–0. Chicago was five outs from the World Series, which the team had not won in 85 years. Florida's Luis Castillo lofted a ball down the leftfield line. Cubs leftfielder Moises Alou leaped, Bartman reached and deflected the ball which fell into the stands. Alou yelled in frustration about the uncaught ball, and Cubs fans, conditioned to expect calamity, sensed impending doom.

Sure enough, Castillo drew a walk, and then the Marlins erupted, scoring eight runs in the inning. The Cubs gave up five hits, three walks and a wild pitch and committed an error, but the heat landed on Bartman—he had to be escorted from Wrigley for his safety. The Marlins won that game, and then the series, and then the World Series after that. Angry Cubs fans drove Bartman into a life of seclusion. He dodged reporters, becoming a media white whale. He notably emerged the summer after Chicago won the World Series in 2016, when the team invited him for a tour of Wrigley and gave him a championship ring. This all happened in private, however. Bartman had seen enough of the spotlight.

Photograph by JOHN BIEVER

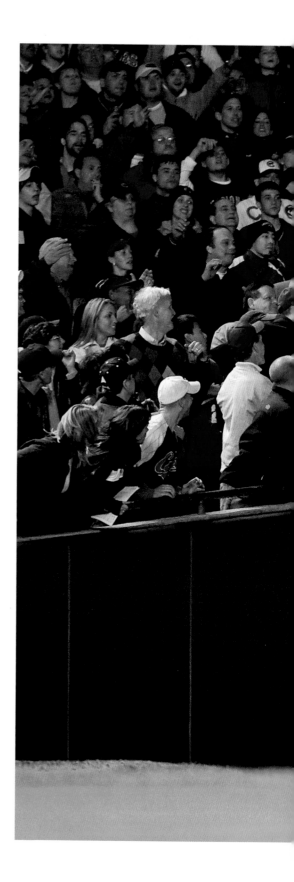

TAINTED TIME

CAPITOL HILL, WASHINGTON, D.C. | *March 17, 2005*

IN 1998 SPORTS ILLUSTRATED named Mark McGwire and Sammy Sosa its Sportsmen of the Year, and a headline above the story declared "Mark McGwire and Sammy Sosa treated the nation to a home run race that was as refreshing as a day at the beach." Soon after, though, fans were feeling burned. In '98 McGwire and Sosa not only chased Roger Maris's single-season home run mark but caught it and beat it into submission with their massive biceps. In real time the chase played as baseball's most entertaining show in ages. But the memory has been robbed of its joy. It now calls to mind a time when accusations against baseball's heroes came in waves and turned the sports pages into a police blotter. McGwire was implicated in the use of performance enhancing drugs by ex-teammate Jose Canseco, himself an admitted user. In 2005 Canseco *(far left)*, Sosa *(center)* and McGwire *(second from near left)* were called before a congressional committee to testify about steroid use. To McGwire's left was Rafael Palmeiro, who hit 569 career home runs and angrily declared to the committee, "I have never used steroids, period!" before being suspended later that season after testing positive for stanozolol. Sosa, reported to have tested positive for PEDs in '03, has steadily denied such charges. McGwire issued many denials before finally admitting, in '10, to steroid use. At the '05 congressional hearings, wanting to avoid perjury charges, McGwire only said, "I'm not here to talk about the past." For many from that era, the past remains an awkward subject.

Photograph by GERALD HERBERT/POOL/GETTY IMAGES

THE SONG BEFORE THE GAME

CAMDEN YARDS, BALTIMORE | *April 4, 2005*

BASEBALL IS AN American game—as American as apple pie and Chevrolet, according to the calculus of a 1970s car advertisement. The game is also where "The Star-Spangled Banner" and sports first became intertwined. During the Cubs–Red Sox World Series of 1918, as the United States was in its second year of fighting in World War I, a live military band performed the song during the seventh-inning stretch at Chicago's Comiskey Park (which the Cubs had rented to accommodate the larger crowd), and the audience began to sing the words. More and more voices joined in and the final words "the home of the brave" were followed by thunderous applause. A *New York Times* report called the performance "the high point of the day's enthusiasm" and the music continued when the Series moved to Boston. From then on live bands regularly performed the anthem at World Series games and on special occasions. The anthem graduated to an every-day, pregame event during World War II, by which time public address systems had been improved to the point that a recording could be broadcast throughout the stadium. The ballplayers removed their caps, and the fans put their hands on their hearts. The patriotic displays escalated after the attacks of Sept. 11, 2001, when Major League Baseball required that teams also play "God Bless America" during the seventh-inning stretch for the rest of the year. Now teams tend to reserve "God Bless America" for Sundays and holidays. But for every game, such as this Orioles Opening Day, "The Star-Spangled Banner" tradition, and our flag, is still there.

Photograph by SIMON BRUTY

"We knew from the start that there was something special about him. The way he carried himself, the way he played the game. He's just all about winning."

—**JOE TORRE**, YANKEES MANAGER

THE YANKEE WAY

YANKEE STADIUM, BRONX, N.Y. | *July 29, 2006*

HE WAS THE Yankees official captain for 12 years, a longer tenure, by a lot, than anyone else, and few players of any generation exhibited so smooth a command of the game and of himself as Derek Sanderson Jeter. In 1996, his first full season with the Yankees, teammates were already gravitating toward him as a leader. That was a year in which Jeter was named Rookie of the Year and batted .361 across three postseason series as the Yankees won their first World Series in two decades. This is an example of related facts. Jeter's Yankees teams won five championships and made the playoffs in all but three seasons of a career that ended in 2014. Jeter grew up in a household in which his mother forbade him to use the word "can't."

He hardly achieved that success alone, of course. Jeter was part of a generation of Yankees-developed stars that included Andy Pettitte, Mariano Rivera and Jorge Posada. But Jeter was the franchise's face and tone-setter. He was selected for 14 All-Star Games, made countless, signature jump throws from shortstop and by the time he retired had played in more games (2,747) and gotten more hits (3,465) than any Yankee ever. Fans remember the moment in the 2001 playoffs against Oakland when Jeter ran from his position to meet a weak throw from rightfield and flip it to catcher Posada for the crucial out. A's GM Billy Beane told SI that he was struck by another play: Late in a regular-season game, the Yankees down, Jeter hit a ground ball and ran to first base in a futile but all-out sprint. The next season Beane showed tape of Jeter's hustle at spring training as an example of how to play the game. It's what Jeter's teammates lived with every day.

Photograph by CHUCK SOLOMON

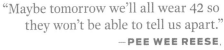

"Maybe tomorrow we'll all wear 42 so
they won't be able to tell us apart."
—PEE WEE REESE,
BROOKLYN DODGERS SHORTSTOP

THE JACKIE IN EVERYONE

DODGER STADIUM, LOS ANGELES | *April 15, 2007*

BASEBALL FIRST BEGAN to honor the special legacy of Jackie Robinson in 1997 when, at a celebration of the 50th anniversary of his breaking of the sport's color barrier, his number 42 was retired around the major leagues. Then, beginning in 2004, baseball declared that every April 15 would be Jackie Robinson Day. "I have often stated that baseball's proudest moment and its most powerful social statement came on April 15, 1947 when Jackie Robinson first set foot on a major league baseball field," said commissioner Bud Selig upon making the announcement. "On that day . . . baseball became the true national pastime." In 2007, the celebration gained a new wrinkle, sparked by an inquiry from Cincinnati Reds outfielder Ken Griffey Jr., who had asked permission to wear number 42 just on April 15. The league approved Griffey's request, applicable to anyone, and more than 150 other players (and some managers and coaches) leaped at the chance to wear Robinson's number for that one special day. The Dodgers among other teams took the idea even further. "Jackie Robinson was a Dodger, and the most fitting tribute the Dodgers can pay to him is for the entire team to wear his number on the 60th anniversary of his breaking the color barrier," team vice chairman and president Jamie McCourt said. The next escalation came on the anniversary date in 2009, when all uniformed personnel on every team wore Robinson's 42—no names on the back of their jerseys, just the number. The annual April 15 celebration now includes special cleats, essay contests and testimonials from players who recognize that, because Robinson went first, they were able to follow.

Photograph by JON SOOHOO/LOS ANGELES DODGERS

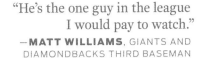

"He's the one guy in the league
I would pay to watch."
—**MATT WILLIAMS**, GIANTS AND
DIAMONDBACKS THIRD BASEMAN

GOING,
GOING, GONE*

AT&T PARK, SAN FRANCISCO | *August 7, 2007*

AT HOME GAMES in San Francisco, fans cheered on Barry Bonds
as he approached the all-time home run record. On the road, it was
another scene. Fans brought CHEATER banners and GOT JUICE signs
and tossed syringes onto the field. No sport cherishes its statistical
records like baseball does, which is why the allegations that Bonds
built his home run totals with the aid of performance enhancing
drugs (the accusations include steroids, human growth hormone,
insulin, testosterone decanoate, bovine steroids and female fertility
drugs) made Bonds a particular target. So many stars of his era—
Roger Clemens, Mark McGwire and Sammy Sosa, to name but
a few—saw their achievements tainted with PED allegations (in
McGwire's case, admitted use), but Bonds was a special case. He
was a second-generation player, the son of Bobby Bonds, godson
of Willie Mays, and he came into the league in 1986 weighing 185
pounds and blessed with enough talent that he won three MVP
awards before he began to add bulk.

In 2007 Bonds was up to 238 pounds, his cap size had allegedly
increased from $7\frac{1}{4}$ to $7\frac{3}{8}$, and he was ready to stage an assault on a
record held by the courageous Hank Aaron. Aaron, of course, took
the title of home run king from the historically beloved Babe Ruth.
This photo shows Bonds hitting his 756th career home run and
seizing the crown, at least in the record books. The home crowd
rose and celebrated—high-fiving, embracing, even tearing up. Aaron
appeared on the big screen with a prerecorded congratulatory
message. By then the debate about Bonds and PEDs, and what it
meant to the authenticity of his record, was already in full throat.

Photograph by BRAD MANGIN

> "If you challenge conventional wisdom, you will find ways to do things much better than they are currently done."
> —**BILL JAMES**, EMPEROR OF BASEBALL STATISTICS

LEADING BY NUMBERS

OAKLAND COLISEUM, OAKLAND | *July 20, 2010*

THE RED SOX were in Oakland for a series when general manager Theo Epstein dropped in on A's counterpart Billy Beane, a little get-together for the men who might be selected one-two if there were ever such a thing as a baseball executives' fantasy draft. Beane, a former player, earned fame as the leading man in *Moneyball*, a book by Michael Lewis (later turned into a somewhat fantastical movie in which Beane was played by Brad Pitt). *Moneyball* chronicled how Beane's Oakland team used breakthrough statistical analysis to identify undervalued players and thus allow a team with a paltry payroll to compete with the league's big spenders. Epstein, a Yale grad, took some of those general *Moneyball* principles and, backed by bigger wallets and ever increasing levels of data analytics, ended two of the most prolonged and commiserated-over title droughts in sports. Epstein was hired to be the Red Sox general manager in 2002 at age 28, and in '04 the team won its first title since 1918; then in 2011 he moved onto Chicago and soon led the Cubs to their first World Series title in 108 years. These hero GMs elevated franchises and revolutionized player evaluation, and they also helped reshape everyday baseball conversations. Before then fans rated players by easily understood statistics that fit neatly on the bottom of a television screen. The Moneyball Era, and the years beyond it, fed fans heaping spoonfuls of alphabet soup: newly emphasized stats included OPS, OPS+, FIP, WAR, oWAR and dWAR. Many slurped it all up. Other fans were just fine talkin' about hits and homers and leaving the alphabet talk to the guys in baseball ops.

Photograph by MICHAEL ZAGARIS

MINOR PLEASURES

GROVE STADIUM, FREDERICK, MARYLAND | *June 22, 2012*

THE MINOR LEAGUES are baseball's fun house. The games don't cost as much. The frisbee-catching dogs who come out between innings can be as much a part of the show as whatever 19-year-old happens to be stepping to the plate. And forget about fan angst. There is no such thing as a long-suffering devotee of the Akron Rubber Ducks. Or the Wichita Wingnuts. Or the Topeka Train Robbers. Wins and losses don't matter so much on the minor league circuit. The show and the atmosphere do.

The minor leagues have been part of baseball almost since the beginning, though the modern "farm system" structure of affiliated teams was created in the 1920s by Branch Rickey's St. Louis Cardinals. For major league teams the minors are about developing talent. For fans it's an opportunity to go to the stadium, maybe ride the carousel (like the one shown here at the Frederick Keys' park), enjoy a sundae and sing along to "Cotton Eye Joe." The stadiums are small enough that every seat is a good one, and the minors are where you find sport's most inventive promotions. For Nobody Night in 2002, the Charleston, S.C. Riverdogs locked out fans until the fifth inning so as to set a record with an official attendance of zero. Since 1997 the Portland (Maine) Sea Dogs have had Field of Dream games in which players, wearing throwback uniforms of the 1926 Portland Eskimos, enter through a faux cornfield. The Altoona Curve held Awful Night, in which fans wore ugly clothes, and the P.A. announcer deliberately mispronounced player names. Go up to Fairbanks on June 21 for the annual Midnight Sun game, hosted by the Alaska Goldpanners. The game starts at 10 p.m. and, thanks to their far-north location, is played in full daylight. That's minor league baseball—always sunny.

Photograph by AL TIELEMANS

AS IT IS WRITTEN

CITIZENS BANK PARK, PHILADELPHIA | *August 5, 2012*

ATHLETES IN EVERY sport sign autographs, but a baseball may
be the ideal physical medium for receiving that signature. The
ball is easy to grip in one hand, and the white background lets the
inscription stand out. The ink makes an impression not just on the
leather, but on the fan who takes that ball home and places it on
a shelf, and every time he looks at it remembers that man in the
uniform writing his name, perhaps an hour or so before first pitch
at the ballpark. Of course there are more mercenary versions of the
autograph encounter. Some players will only sign for those who
pay a fee and stand in line at a memorabilia show. Then there's
the "fan" whose signed balls will be up for sale on eBay before the
game has reached its seventh-inning stretch.

Still it's heartening—and hearkening, to a great baseball
tradition—that many stars still take time before the game to
wade into the sea of outstretched arms and sign for as long as
they can. Ryan Howard, the player in this photo, had his ups and
downs during his years with the Phillies. He began his career
with a Rookie of the Year award in 2005 and National League
MVP honors in '06. Later, his contract numbers ballooned, and
his plate statistics dwindled. But even when the local sports talk
radio conversations had turned against him, he remained an
accommodating signer, aware of his stature and grateful for the
fans. The pen was willing, even when the bat no longer was.

Photograph by BRIAN GARFINKEL/GETTY IMAGES

A GIRL AMONG BOYS

SOUTH WILLIAMSPORT, PENNSYLVANIA | *August 15, 2014*

AT THE AGE OF 13, she had a confidence that she had picked up not only on the diamond, but also on the soccer field and the basketball court, where she had regularly dominated boys her age. Mo'ne Davis was first recruited to organized competition when a coach saw her in a city park, at age seven, throwing perfect football spirals and was impressed by her athleticism. For years the sports fields had taught this girl that "anything they can do, I can do better."

By the time of the 2014 Little League World Series she was 5' 4" and 111 pounds, and in regard to size she looked like an average member of the otherwise all-male Taney Dragons of Philadelphia. What set Mo'ne apart, beyond her gender, was her 70-mile-per-hour fastball and her slippery curve. In the first game of the tournament she unleashed her talents on the boys from Nashville, who were left scoreless as Davis struck out eight, walked none, and became the first girl to earn a win and pitch a shutout in the history of the Series. She became an instant celebrity, a model for aspiring girls everywhere. She pitched Wiffle balls to Jimmy Fallon on his late-night talk show, met President Barack Obama and his wife Michelle, and put a spin move on comedian Kevin Hart in the celebrity game at the '15 NBA All-Star Weekend at Madison Square Garden. People fell over themselves to celebrate her achievement and show that sports are for everyone. As Mo'ne would say in the aftermath: "Throwing 70 miles an hour—*that's* throwing like a girl."

Photograph by AL TIELEMANS

ENERGY, UNBOUNDED

BUSCH STADIUM, ST. LOUIS | *August 31, 2015*

BASEBALL REGENERATES ITSELF. Cobb and Ruth are replaced by Williams and Mays, who give way to Rose and Ripken and Jeter, and then along comes Bryce Harper. This prodigal talent sprouted early. Growing up in Las Vegas, he passed his GED test and began playing junior college ball at age 16. At 19 he was playing outfield for the Washington Nationals, and the youngest guy on the field was owning it. After winning Rookie of the Year in 2012 he articulated his ball-playing philosophy: "I'm going to run as hard as I can, hit the ball as hard as I can and swing as hard as I can every time." Harper has lived up to that credo, sometimes to his detriment. He's twice injured himself running into outfield walls, and he once sprained his thumb diving headfirst into third on a bases-clearing triple. But when fully healthy in '15, he

had a season for the ages: 42 home runs, a .330 average, a majors-best 1.109 OPS and his first MVP award, at age 22.

Harper's numbers invite comparisons to the stars of yesteryear, but in some ways he is a man of these times. His hairstyle changes often, and in interesting ways. He's emotional on the field, jawing with umpires. In a 2016 interview with ESPN, he called baseball "a tired sport, because you can't express yourself. You can't do what people in other sports do. I'm not saying baseball is, you know, boring or anything like that, but it's the excitement of the young guys who are coming into the game now who have flair." The comments are part of the process of regeneration. Youth will have its say.

Photograph by JEFF ROBERSON/AP

THE WEIGHT IS LIFTED

PROGRESSIVE FIELD, CLEVELAND | *November 2, 2016*

AFTER WINNING BACK-TO-BACK World Series in 1907 and '08, the Cubs lost in the Series in '10 but surely figured, How far off could the next title be? The Cubs did reach the World Series again—six times, up through 1945—but they never won one and the wait, after a certain point, became the stuff of gallows humor, a catalog of cursed moments and some near misses, a reason to shrug in the City with Broad Shoulders. The Red Sox had ended their own 86-year drought in 2004. When would Chicago's turn come?

In Game 7 of the '16 World Series against Cleveland, the Cubs held a three-run lead with two outs in the eighth inning when the Indians rallied to tie. But this time, when it all seemed to be going wrong, Chicago benefited from divine intervention in the form of a 17-minute rain delay that gave the reeling Cubs an opportunity to regroup. They did, scoring two runs in the 10th, going ahead on Ben Zobrist's RBI double. In the bottom of the inning, third baseman Kris Bryant fielded a two-out ground ball and threw to Anthony Rizzo at first, and Chicago's 108-year wait, the longest interim between titles known to man, was over. "Right now," Dave Martinez, a Cubs bench coach and former player, told SI then, "I think about the parents and the grandparents—all the people who waited for this day and the many of them who never lived to see it." The victory parade was attended by five million people (nearly twice the '16 population of Chicago), according to city estimates. That number, if accurate, would make it not only the biggest sports celebration ever, but also one of history's biggest gatherings of humanity. Cubs fans had to be there. Who knew when such a moment might come again?

Photograph by EZRA SHAW/GETTY IMAGES

GOOD PITCH, GOOD HIT

ANGEL STADIUM, ANAHEIM
May 20, 2018

NOT SINCE 1919. Not since Babe Ruth. These phrases encapsulated the wonder of Shohei Ohtani, the kind of player fans never thought they would see. The two-way threat—a guy good enough to dominate games as a pitcher, and also good enough to be a force in the lineup as a batter on his nonpitching days—recalled baseball's early decades. Yet it didn't happen much even back then. It's too hard to do. Then in 2018 a long, lean 23-year-old came from Japan to America to play for the Los Angeles Angels with double duty on his mind.

Ohtani had played both ways in the Japan League, and when the Angels gave him the chance, it worked. On the days he wasn't throwing 100 mph fastballs, Ohtani was crushing home runs with an exit velocity as searing as his pitch speed. He excelled from the start, which is especially impressive considering he was not only attempting a historic feat but also adjusting to a new culture and to the peculiarities

of the American game, with its higher mound and different baseball seams. None of this seemed to bother him. Angels pitching coach Charles Nagy was asked what stood out about Ohtani and answered, "His enthusiasm. He works hard and when he leaves he studies hard. He loves everything about baseball." Home attendance was up for games when fans knew Ohtani would be on the mound.

There was always the risk that the good times would not last—and an injury to Ohtani's elbow dampened things in his first season. Still, these were momentous days. Baseball caught fire in Japan when Ruth led an All-Star team on an exhibition there in 1934. So there's a bit of poetry in that country's sending the modern version of the Babe to American shores.

Photographs by JAYNE KAMIN-ONCEA/ GETTY IMAGES *(left) and* JOHN CORDES/ ICON SPORTSWIRE/GETTY IMAGES

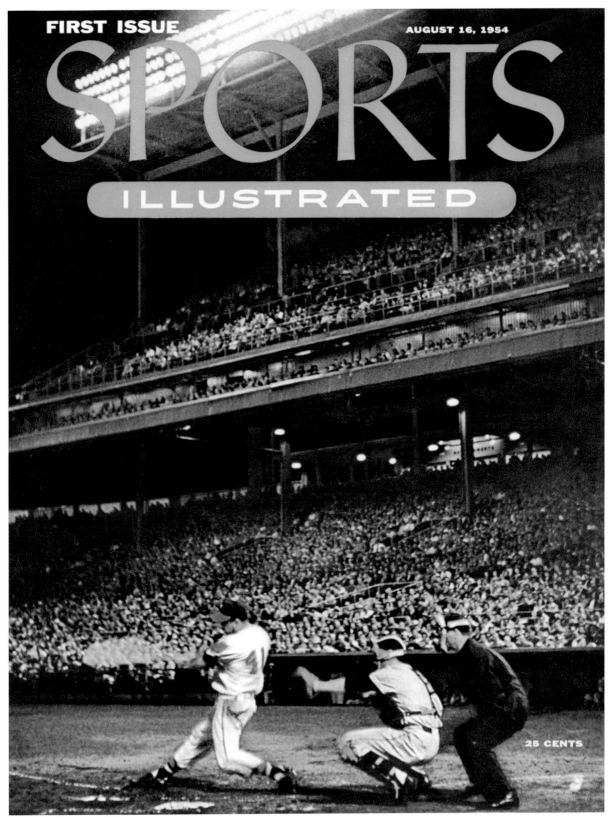

FIRST ISSUE

AUGUST 16, 1954

SPORTS

ILLUSTRATED

25 CENTS

EDDIE MATHEWS
August 16, 1954

YOGI BERRA
July 11, 1955

COVERING THE BASES

The 100 Greatest Baseball Covers of All Time

OVER ITS 65-PLUS YEARS, SPORTS ILLUSTRATED has produced more than 3,250 national magazine covers. The covers have depicted dozens of disparate disciplines. Football and fencing. Skiing and swimming. Dog breeding and deep-sea diving. Basketball, ballooning, bird-watching and boxing. And, of course, baseball. The national pastime graced SI's first-ever cover in the summer of 1954. (The Milwaukee Braves were chasing the pennant, their lefty slugger Eddie Mathews was en route to a 40-home run season, the ballpark was handsomely packed.) And baseball has been the primary subject of some 650 covers since. That's about one out of every five.

Baseball, more than any other sport, evolves and thrives partly in relation to a rich, resonant history. So does SPORTS ILLUSTRATED. That's why, as we selected our 100 greatest baseball covers we were careful to represent each year at least once. Each season in the intertwined life of the sport and the magazine matters, and each in its way leads to the next. Some baseball folks have been out front more than once. A lot more. Pete Rose holds 22 major league records—and also holds the distinction of appearing on 15 SI covers, more than any other baseball player, outdistancing another switch-hitter, Mickey Mantle, and a modern pillar, Derek Jeter, each of whom have been on 13.

What makes a great cover anyway? An arresting image surely helps (Tony Conigliaro's blackened eye in 1970, say, or Jay Buhner and his two-year-old son biting a bat in '96). Or big news (Hank Aaron with the simple and powerful "715" above him in '74), or something seismic being revealed (STEROIDS IN BASEBALL in 2002). And while cleverness coupled with an image can leave its happy mark (YOGI'S BACK! in 1984), sometimes the right photograph at the right moment needs no words at all (the boyish, black-and-white portrait of Mantle after his death in '95). All in all, settling upon just 100 covers—tossing aside five or six for each one that we chose—was a difficult assignment. There's not one of those 650-plus after all that didn't feel like a great cover on the day the editors were putting it out. The ones finally selected, we hope, each have an especially enduring quality: a great cover at first glance, that becomes greater still the longer you look at it.

TED WILLIAMS
August 1, 1955

MICKEY MANTLE
June 18, 1956

WARREN SPAHN
June 25, 1956

WORLD SERIES
September 30, 1957

YANKEES AT SPRING TRAINING
March 3, 1958

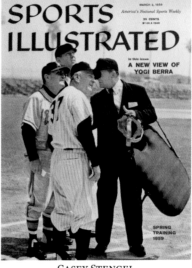

CASEY STENGEL
March 2, 1959

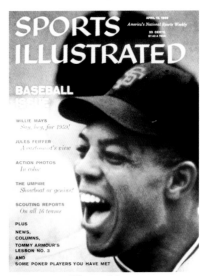

WILLIE MAYS
April 13, 1959

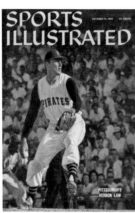

VERNON LAW
October 10, 1960

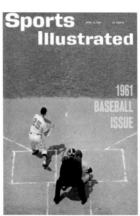

BASEBALL PREVIEW
April 10, 1961

CASEY STENGEL
March 5, 1962

LUIS APARICIO
April 30, 1962

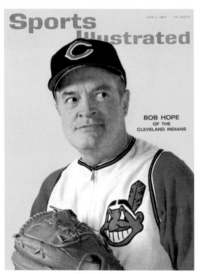

BOB HOPE
June 3, 1963

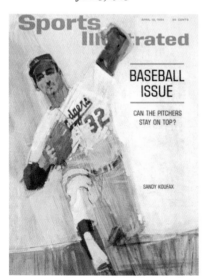

SANDY KOUFAX
April 13, 1964

JUAN MARICHAL
August 9, 1965

CURT FLOOD
August 19, 1968

TONY OLIVA
August 23, 1965

JOE MORGAN AND SONNY JACKSON
June 6, 1966

THE O'S ROBINSONS
October 10, 1966

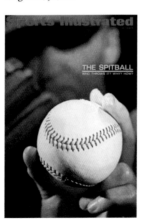

THE SPITBALL
July 31, 1967

CARL YASTRZEMSKI
August 21, 1967

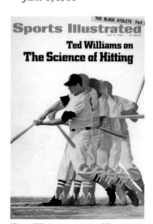

TED WILLIAMS ON HITTING
July 8, 1968

BILL FREEHAN
April 14, 1969

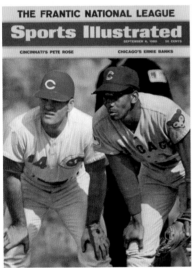
PETE ROSE AND ERNIE BANKS
September 8, 1969

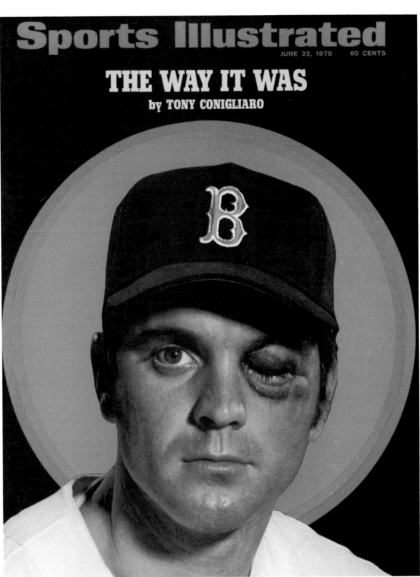
TONY CONIGLIARO
June 22, 1970

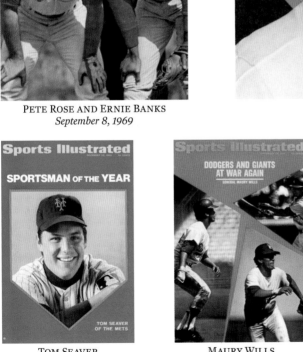
TOM SEAVER
December 22, 1969

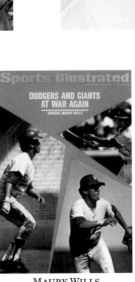
MAURY WILLS
September 27, 1971

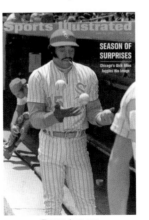
DICK ALLEN
June 12, 1972

WORLD SERIES
October 22, 1973

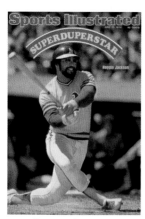

REGGIE JACKSON
June 17, 1974

PETE ROSE
December 22, 1975

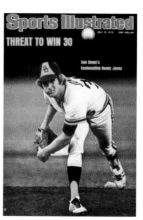

RANDY JONES
July 12, 1976

MARK FIDRYCH
June 6, 1977

HANK AARON
April 15, 1974

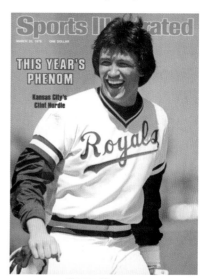

CLINT HURDLE
March 20, 1978

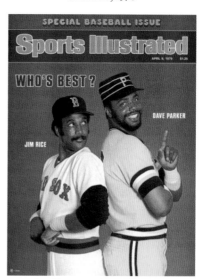

JIM RICE AND DAVE PARKER
April 9, 1979

KEITH HERNANDEZ
April 7, 1980

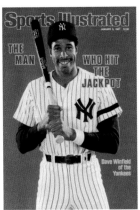

DAVE WINFIELD
January 5, 1981

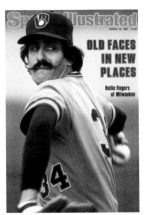

ROLLIE FINGERS
March 16, 1981

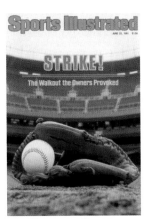

BASEBALL STRIKE
June 22, 1981

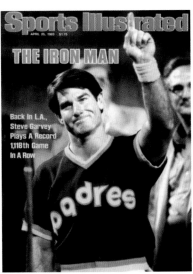

STEVE GARVEY
April 25, 1983

ROD CAREW
June 13, 1983

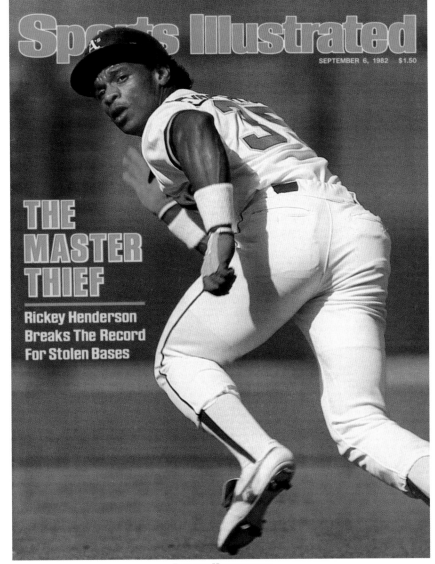

RICKEY HENDERSON
September 6, 1982

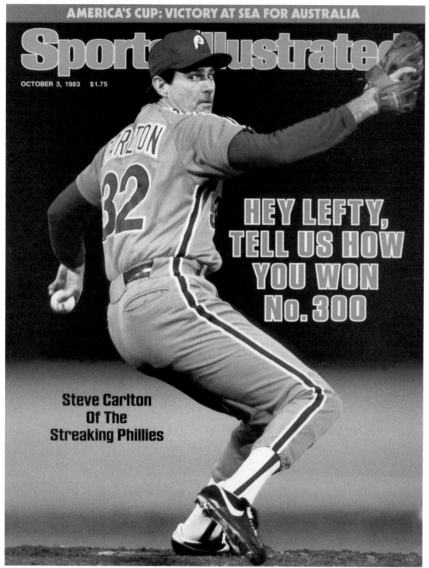

STEVE CARLTON
October 3, 1983

ANDRE DAWSON AND DAVE STIEB
July 18, 1983

YOGI BERRA
April 2, 1984

OZZIE SMITH
October 28, 1985

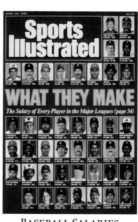

DARRYL STRAWBERRY
October 6, 1986

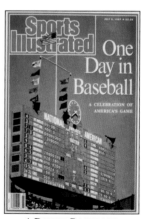

BASEBALL SALARIES
April 20, 1987

A DAY IN BASEBALL
July 6, 1987

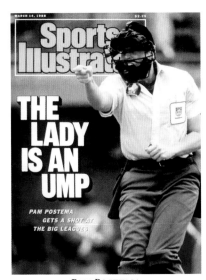

PAM POSTEMA
March 14, 1988

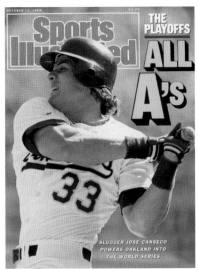

JOSE CANSECO
October 17, 1988

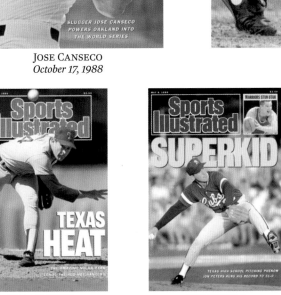

KEN GRIFFEY JR.
May 7, 1990

NOLAN RYAN
May 1, 1989

JON PETERS
May 8, 1989

BO JACKSON
June 12, 1989

EARTHQUAKE AT SERIES
October 30, 1989

 OREL HERSHISER
July 1, 1991

KIRBY PUCKETT
April 6, 1992

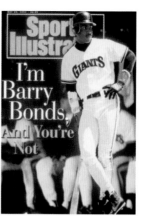

BARRY BONDS
May 24, 1993

GIBSON AND MCLAIN
July 19, 1993

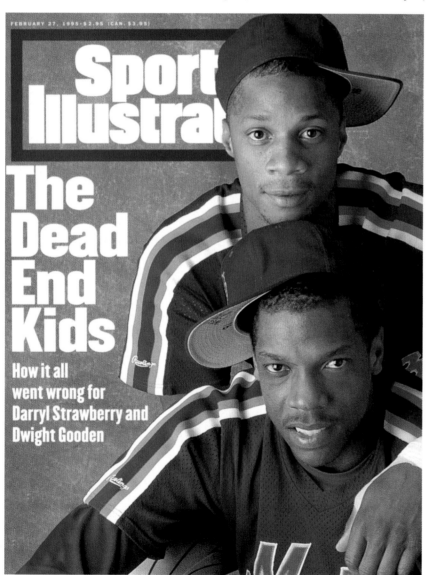

DARRYL STRAWBERRY AND DWIGHT GOODEN
February 27, 1995

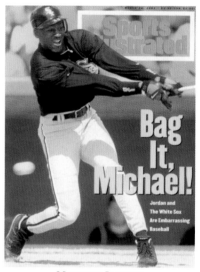

MICHAEL JORDAN
March 14, 1994

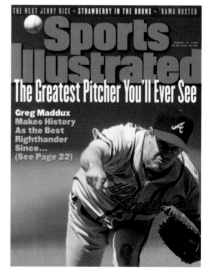

GREG MADDUX
August 14, 1995

MICKEY MANTLE
August 21, 1995

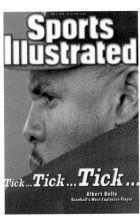

ALBERT BELLE
May 6, 1996

MARGE SCHOTT
May 20, 1996

RODRIGUEZ AND JETER
February 24, 1997

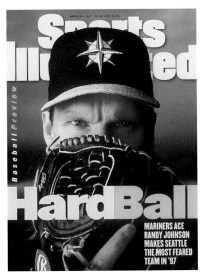

RANDY JOHNSON
March 31, 1997

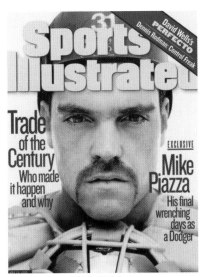

MIKE PIAZZA
May 25, 1998

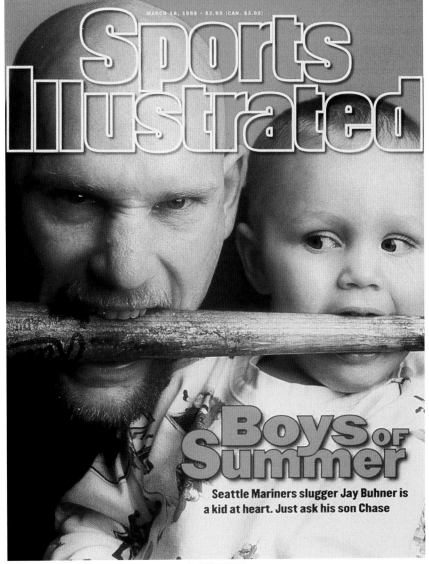

JAY BUHNER
March 18, 1996

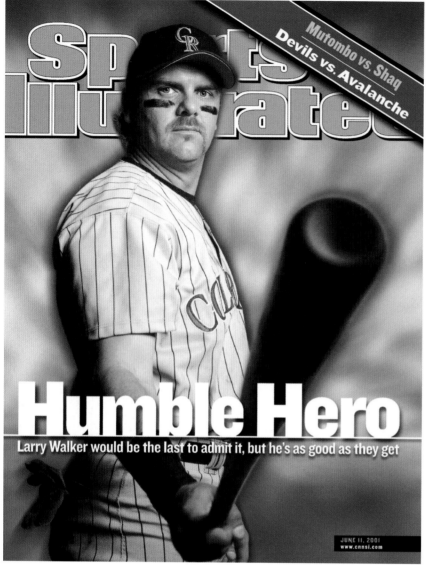

LARRY WALKER
June 11, 2001

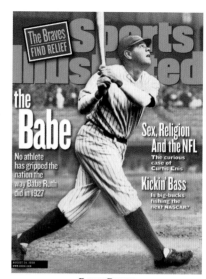

BABE RUTH
August 24, 1998

MARK MCGWIRE AND SAMMY SOSA
December 21, 1998

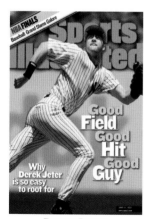

DEREK JETER
June 21, 1999

JASON GIAMBI
July 17, 2000

NOMAR GARCIAPARRA
March 5, 2001

DIAMONDBACKS WIN SERIES
November 12, 2001

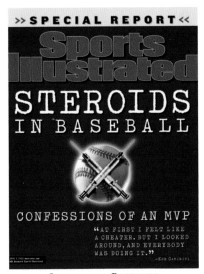

STEROIDS IN BASEBALL
June 3, 2002

KERRY WOOD AND MARK PRIOR
July 7, 2003

BARRY BONDS
August 13, 2007

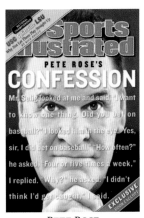

PETE ROSE
January 12, 2004

RED SOX FANS MOSAIC
December 6, 2004

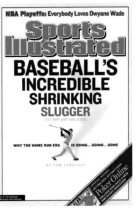

HOME RUN DECLINE
May 30, 2005

ALBERT PUJOLS
May 22, 2006

BIZARRO BASEBALL
May 26, 2008

TIM LINCECUM
July 7, 2008

BRYCE HARPER
June 8, 2009

JIM THOME
September 27, 2010

DEREK JETER, JORGE POSADA, MARIANO RIVERA AND ANDY PETTITTE
May 3, 2010

JOE DiMAGGIO
May 14, 2011

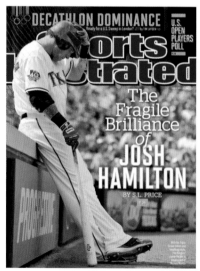

JOSH HAMILTON
June 11, 2012

MARIANO RIVERA
September 23, 2013

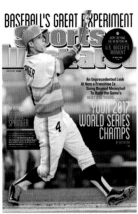

ASTROS PREDICTION
June 30, 2014

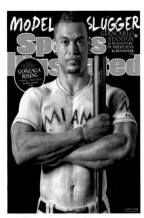

GIANCARLO STANTON
March 2, 2015

KRIS BRYANT
November 14, 2016

THE CURVEBALL
May 29, 2017

MONE DAVIS
August 25, 2014

MIKE TROUT AND SHOHEI OHTANI
March 26, 2018

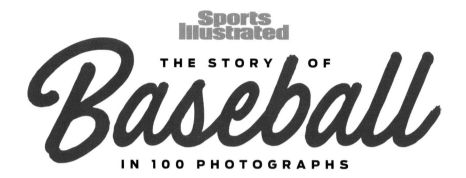

Sports Illustrated

THE STORY OF
Baseball
IN 100 PHOTOGRAPHS

ADDITIONAL PHOTO CREDITS

FRONT COVER: John Dominis/The LIFE Picture Collection/Getty Images. BACK COVER *(clockwise from top left)*: Charles M. Conlon/ Sporting News Archive/Getty Images, Tony Triolo, Walter Iooss Jr. FRONT FLAP: Jon SooHoo/Los Angeles Dodgers. BACK FLAP: Jeff Roberson/AP. Page 6: Courtesy of the Boston Public Library/Leslie Jones Collection. Pages 8-9: Sarony, Major & Knapp Lith./Library of Congress. Pages 10-11: Chicago History Museum/Getty Images. Page 12: Heinz Kluetmeier. Page 15: Bret Wills. Page 37: Bret Wills. Page 73: David N. Berkwitz. Page 121: Bret Wills. Page 177: Milo Stewart/National Baseball Hall of Fame Library. Pages 224-239: Mark Bagley, Karl Story and Alex Sinclair; Robert Beck (2), Jon Brenneis, Tom Dahlin, Jonathan Daniel/Allsport, James Drake (3), Bill Frakes, Bernie Fuchs, Otto Greule Jr/Getty Images, John Iacono (5), Walter Iooss Jr. (16), Fred Kaplan, Mark Kauffman (5), Heinz Kluetmeier (3), Neil Leifer (5), George Long, V.J. Lovero (3), Richard Mackson (4), Brad Mangin, John W. McDonough, Richard Meek, Manny Millan (2), Ronald C. Modra (5), National Baseball Hall of Fame/Reuters, Peter Newcomb/Reuters, Greg Nelson (2), Marvin E. Newman, Michael O'Neill, Hy Peskin (4), James Porto, Mike Powell, Herb Scharfman, Art Shay, George Silk/The LIFE Picture Collection/Getty Images, Robert Silvers/www.photomosaic.com, Don Smith, William R. Smith, Chuck Solomon (3), Lane Stewart (3), Al Tielemans (3), Transcendental Graphics/Getty Images, Tony Triolo, John G. Zimmerman (6).

Special thanks to Prem Kalliat, Will Welt, George Amores, Gerry Burke, Sandra Vallejos, Brian Mai, Beth Bugler, Liana Zamora, Stephen Skalocky, Mark Bechtel, Stephen Cannella, Gabe Miller and Susan Szeliga from the SI universe; Anja Schmidt, Gary Stewart, Hillary Leary, Elizabeth Austin, Alex Voznesenskiy, Gina Scauzillo, Suzanne Albert, Danielle Costa and Tom Maloney of Time Inc. Books; John Horne, Kelli Bogan and Matt Rothenberg at the National Baseball Hall of Fame; Rosemary Lavery of the Boston Public Library; Bill Hooper at the New York Historical Society Library; Bob Cullum and Michael Nola.

ISBN: 978-1-5478-0013-1
Library of Congress Control Number: 2018949730
First edition, 2018
1 QGV 18
10 9 8 7 6 5 4 3 2 1

We welcome your comments and suggestions about Time Inc. Books. Please write to us at: Time Inc. Books, Attention: Book Editors, P.O. Box 62310, Tampa, FL 33662-2310 • (800) 765-6400 • timeincbooks.com. • Time Inc. Books products may be purchased for business or promotional use. For information on bulk purchases, please contact Christi Crowley in the Special Sales Department at (845) 895-9858.

FENWAY PARK, BOSTON | *April 29, 2017*